Bhagavad Gita

(in English)

~

The Authentic English Translation for Accurate and Unbiased Understanding

~

HARI CHETAN

Copyright © Hari Chetan 2021

All rights reserved. No part of this publication may be reproduced or transmitted in any form or by any means, electronic, mechanical, photocopying, recording, scanning, or otherwise, without written permission from the author. It is illegal to copy this book, post it to a website, or distribute it by any other means without permission.

Disclaimers: This book is intended to provide accurate information concerning the subject matter covered. However, the author and the publisher accept no responsibility for inaccuracies or omissions, and the author and the publisher specifically disclaim any liability, loss, or risk, whether personal, financial, or otherwise, that is incurred as a result, directly or indirectly, from the use and/or application of the contents of this book.

Moreover, the author and the publisher of this book do not intend to hurt the sentiments of anyone, including any religion, ethnic group, caste, creed, sect, organization, company, and individual. They respect all religions and ideologies and accept no responsibility if anyone is hurt by the contents of this book.

Note: Throughout this book, the author has used the masculine gender only for ease in writing and such use is not intended to undermine the feminine gender or a third gender by any means. The principles and methods discussed in this book apply to all genders equally.

A Gift for You

In the daily commotion that characterizes our lives nowadays, it is quite easy to lose track of oneself. And so it is important for us to maintain our mental equilibrium by connecting with our spiritual selves on a regular basis.

Download Hari Chetan's **free Bhagavad Gita Workbook** designed especially for the readers of his books.

This workbook will help you test your knowledge of the core concepts given in the Bhagavad Gita, and to keep you on track in your spiritual journey.

Try it. It's free to download and is very useful!

Visit **www.harichetan.com** to download.

Thoughts of Intellectuals on the Bhagavad Gita

"When doubts haunt me, when disappointments stare me in the face, and I see not one ray of hope on the horizon, I turn to Bhagavad Gita and find a verse to comfort me; and I immediately begin to smile in the midst of overwhelming sorrow. Those who meditate on the Gita will derive fresh joy and new meanings from it every day." ~ Mahatma Gandhi

"The marvel of the Bhagavad Gita is its truly beautiful revelation of life's wisdom which enables philosophy to blossom into religion." ~ Hermann Hesse

"(The Bhagavad Gita is) one of the most clear and comprehensive summaries of perennial philosophy ever revealed; hence its enduring value is subject not only to India but to all of humanity." ~ Aldous Huxley

"That the spiritual man need not be a recluse, that union with the divine life may be achieved and maintained in the midst of worldly affairs, that the obstacles to that union lie not outside us but within us — such is the central lesson of the Bhagavad Gita." ~ Annie Besant

"In the morning I bathe my intellect in the stupendous and cosmogonal philosophy of the Bhagavad Gita in comparison with which our modern world and its literature seem puny and trivial." ~ Henry David Thoreau

"I owed a magnificent day to the Bhagavad Gita. It was as if an empire spoke to us, nothing small or unworthy, but large, serene, consistent, the voice of an old intelligence which in another age and climate had pondered and thus disposed of the same questions which exercise us." ~ Ralph Waldo Emerson

"Bhagavad Gita is a true scripture of the human race, a living creation rather than a book, with a new message for every age and a new meaning for every civilization." ~ Sri Aurobindo

"The most beautiful, perhaps the only true philosophical song existing in any known tongue … perhaps the deepest and loftiest thing the world has to show." ~ Wilhelm von Humboldt

"I am 90% through the Bhagavad Gita … My inner Arjuna is being channelled." ~ Will Smith

"The Bhagavad Gita deals essentially with the spiritual foundation of human existence. It is a call of action to meet the obligations and duties of life; yet keeping in view the spiritual nature and grander purpose of the universe." ~ Jawaharlal Nehru

"I hesitate not to pronounce the Gita a performance of great originality, of sublimity of conception, reasoning and diction almost unequalled; and a single exception, amongst all the known religions of mankind." ~ Lord Warren Hastings

"Those are spiritual things to reflect upon yourself, life, the world around you and see things the other way. I thought it (the Bhagavad Gita) was quite appropriate." ~ Sunita Williams

The Bhagavad Gita Series

Book 1: Bhagavad Gita - The Perfect Philosophy: 15 Reasons That Make the Song of God the Most Scientific Ideology

Book 2: Bhagavad Gita (in English): The Authentic English Translation for Accurate and Unbiased Understanding

Book 3: 30 Days to Understanding the Bhagavad Gita: A Complete, Simple, and Step-by-Step Guide to the Million-Year-Old Confidential Knowledge

Book 4: The Bhagavad Gita Summarized and Simplified: A Comprehensive and Easy-to-Read Summary of the Divine Song of God

Book 5: Mind Management through the Bhagavad Gita: Master your Mindset in 21 Days and Discover Unlimited Happiness and Success

All Books: Bhagavad Gita (In English) – The Complete Collection: 5-Books-in-1

DEDICATED TO

The Seekers of Truth

"To you, who does not carp, I shall now impart this most confidential knowledge and realization, knowing which you shall be liberated from evil."

[Lord Krishna to Arjuna - Bhagavad Gita 9.1]

Names of Lord Krishna mentioned in the Bhagavad Gita

Achyuta — The infallible one; One who is changeless
Devesha — The Lord of lords
Govinda — One who gives pleasure to the cows; Knower of the activities of the senses
Hari — The absorber of all sorrows and pains; Lord of nature
Hrishikesha — The Lord of the senses
Janardana — One who afflicts felons; The one who grants the prayers of devotees
Keshava — The slayer of demon Keshi; One with long, beautiful hair
Krishna — The all-attractive one; Dark complexioned one
Madhava — The husband of Laxmi, the goddess of fortune
Madhusudana — The slayer of demon Madhu
Purushuttama — The best of all men; The supreme person
Varshneya — Descendant of Vrishni
Vasudeva — The Lord; Son of Vasudeva
Vishnu — The all-pervading Lord
Vishwamurte — The form of the entire universe
Yadava — Descendant of Yadu

Names of Arjuna mentioned in the Bhagavad Gita

Anagha — One who is sinless
Arjuna — One who is pure or white
Dhananjaya — Winner of wealth

Gudakesha — Conqueror of sleep
Kaunteya — Son of Kunti
Kiriti — The one who dones the glorious crown given by Indra
Mahabaho — Mighty-armed one
Pandava — Son of Pandu
Parantapa — Scorcher of enemies
Partha — Son of Pritha (Kunti)
Savyasachi — An archer capable of shooting even with the left hand

Table of Contents

Introduction 19
   A brief history of the Bhagavad Gita...................21
   The magic of the Bhagavad Gita.........................26
   Why did the Lord sing the Bhagavad Gita? 28
   Bhagavad Gita — A guide beyond religion.........30
   How is this book different?.................................31
   A note to the reader (Important) 32
Chapter 1 - Arjuna's Grief 35
Chapter 2 - An Introduction to Yoga 47
Chapter 3 - The Yoga of Action...................................67
Chapter 4 - The Yoga of Knowledge 79
Chapter 5 - True Renunciation 91
Chapter 6 - The Yoga of Meditation 99
Chapter 7 - The Supreme and His Nature 111
Chapter 8 - The Imperishable Supreme.....................119
Chapter 9 - The Royal Secret 127
Chapter 10 - The Glories of the Divine One..............137
Chapter 11 - The Universal Form of God 147
Chapter 12 - The Yoga of Devotion 161
Chapter 13 - The Nature and the Soul 167
Chapter 14 - The Three Modes of Material Nature...177
Chapter 15 - The Supreme Person 185
Chapter 16 - Divine and Demonic Natures 191
Chapter 17 - The Three Kinds of Faith......................197
Chapter 18 - Renunciation and Liberation 205
Conclusion 225
About the Author...229

Introduction

When he enters this world, a living being's mind is blank, except for the recollections of being kept within a cage for several weeks or months. Then his learning process begins gradually. Throughout his life, he keeps learning from various sources — family, teachers, friends, strangers, the environment, nature, books, television, movies, the internet, and whatnot. But there always remains a large knowledge gap that needs to be filled. None of these sources of knowledge gives him an insight into *himself*. At all times, he identifies himself with a face, a gender, an address, a city, and a country. If he obtains a degree and a professional designation, he begins to associate himself with those qualifications and titles. All his life he thinks himself to be the child of his parents, the husband of his wife, the father of his children, and so on. However, that void is never filled, because none of these is his true identity.

Most of us never ask ourselves who we truly are, where we came from and for what, where we will go once we die, and other similar questions about our identity. It's true that at some point in our lives, we all face these questions. However, we have no idea where to find the answers and are too busy to keep looking. So, we don't bother much.

The Bhagavad Gita has all of those answers.

The Bhagavad Gita is a book of open secrets. 'Open' because we all have access to it. 'Secret' because most of us do not care to expose ourselves to that knowledge. And many of those who do enter this magnificent pool of wisdom do not receive much out of it, all because they were expecting a quick fix mantra that would solve all of their problems instantaneously.

The Bhagavad Gita is the comprehensive instruction manual provided by God to us for living a perfect life in this material world.

Even after reading over a hundred books on the subject, I haven't been able to define the Bhagavad Gita in one sentence any better than this. Over the past decade, I've tried to come up with a comprehensive definition of the Bhagavad Gita; but every time I tried, the definition grew into a one-page synopsis. I eventually concluded that the only way to comprehend Gita properly is to read it from beginning to end. There are no sets of words that can adequately express the depths of knowledge it contains.

Before we get into the magnificence of the Bhagavad Gita, let me present a brief historical backdrop of what led to the situation when God Himself sung His divine song to His devotee for the benefit of all humanity.

A brief history of the Bhagavad Gita

In the ancient Kuru dynasty of Hastinapur, appeared King Shantanu. He had a wife named Ganga. As an after-effect of a curse by Brahma, Ganga had to leave Shantanu. They had a son named Devavrata, who was gifted in every way. Shantanu fell in love with Satyavati, a fisherman's adopted daughter, and wished to marry her. Her father, however, approved of the marriage on the condition that Satyavati's son inherits the Hastinapur crown. When Devavrata learned of this, he gave up his right to the throne and made a vow to never marry and to serve the throne until the end of his days. Devavrata thus earned the name Bhishma (one who has taken a terrible vow).

One of the sons of Shantanu and Satyavati, named Vichitravirya, inherited the throne from his father. He had two wives named Ambika and Ambalika. Ambika gave birth to a son named Dhritarashtra, and Ambalika had a son named Pandu. Because Dhritarashtra was born blind, his stepbrother Pandu, though younger than him, ascended to the throne. Dhritarashtra saw this as an injustice to himself. He married Gandhari and had a hundred sons and one daughter with her. Duryodhana was the eldest of their children. Dhritarashtra had another son with his second wife, Vaishya, named Yuyutsu. Pandu also married twice and had three sons, Yudhisthira, Bhima, and Arjuna, from his first wife Kunti, and two sons, Nakula and Sahadeva, from his second wife Madri.

Pandu died young, and thereafter Dhritarashtra became the king, much to his delight. His sons, called the Kauravas, despised their cousins, the sons of Pandu, known as the Pandavas. When they grew up, the kingdom was divided into two halves, with the fertile half going to the Kauravas and the infertile half going to the Pandavas. The Pandavas, however, used their skills and the help of their cousin Krishna to transform the barren region into a heavenly empire. When Duryodhana visited their kingdom, Indraprastha, he became very envious.

Duryodhana even attempted to kill the five sons of Pandu, as well as Kunti, by burning them alive. But with the help of Krishna, who happened to be Kunti's nephew, the Pandavas and Kunti were able to escape.

Then Duryodhana invited his cousins to a 'friendly' game of gambling. Duryodhana cheated at the game with the help of his uncle Shakuni and took everything from the Pandavas, including Draupadi, their wife. Duryodhana even tried to strip Draupadi in front of everyone. Draupadi, however, was saved by Krishna. Duryodhana ordered that the Pandavas serve thirteen years in the woods including one year in anonymity. The rules were designed in such a way that if the Pandavas were discovered in the final year, they would have to start over.

When the Pandavas returned after the completion of the term and demanded their kingdom back, Duryodhana refused, claiming that they were identified in the final year and so they needed to repeat the thirteen-year sentence.

War remained the only option for the Pandavas. Arjuna, the third of the Pandava brothers and the best archer in the world, and Duryodhana went to see Krishna and ask for his assistance. As fate would have it, they both left at the same time. Duryodhana was the first to arrive. Krishna was sound asleep at the time, and Duryodhana stood by His head, waiting for Him to awaken. Arjuna arrived a few minutes later and, seeing Krishna sleeping, reverently stood by His feet. Because Arjuna was the first person that Krishna saw when He awoke, much to Duryodhana's annoyance, tradition mandated that Krishna accept Arjuna's request first. He declared that one side could have His army and the other could have Him. He, however, made it clear that He would not take part in the upcoming war as a king or warrior. Duryodhana was aware of Krishna's vast military forces and was enraged that Arjuna had been given the choice first. However, he was surprised and delighted when Arjuna chose Krishna over His military troops. Knowing Krishna's true identity, Arjuna was content to have his Lord on his side, regardless of whether He fought or not. He requested Krishna to be his charioteer and guide in the great war, which Krishna pleasantly agreed to.

Dhritarashtra, being blind, could not participate in the war. However, out of concern for his sons, the Kauravas, he wished to know what was going on on the battlefield in real time. Sage Ved Vyasa, an avatar of Lord Vishnu, granted divine eyes to his disciple and Dhritarashtra's charioteer, Sanjaya, so that he could see the happenings of the battle and narrate the same to Dhritarashtra.

All armies assembled on the great battlefield of Kurukshetra. When the war was about to begin, Arjuna asked Krishna to draw up his chariot in between the two vast armies, so that he could see who all had gathered to fight in this great battle. As he surveyed both sides, he saw friends and family all around. Standing opposite him were his cousins, the sons of his uncle, Dhritarashtra.

Present also was his military teacher Drona, for whom he has a great deal of respect. The opposing armies were led by Bhishma, the great-grandsire of the Kuru dynasty, who had lavished love on all the Pandava princes, especially Arjuna. Bhishma had to take Duryodhana's side, as he had pledged to remain a servant of the throne all his life. Arjuna then saw many other friends and relatives standing on both sides, ready to fight. Overcome by love and compassion for his loved ones, Arjuna slumped down on his chariot, and perplexed about the right course of action, asked Krishna to be his spiritual guide and to advise him.

Noticing Arjuna's bewilderment, Lord Krishna transformed into his spiritual master and sang to him His divine song, the Bhagavad Gita, enlightening him about the greatest truths in the universe and dispelling all his doubts and fears.

This divine conversation was recorded in writing by Veda Vyasa in the form of 700 verses (or 701 verses, depending on the way the Sanskrit verses are grouped), separated into 18 chapters. The Bhagavad Gita forms chapters 23 to 40 of Book VI of the Mahabharata.

The magic of the Bhagavad Gita

I call the Bhagavad Gita the "end of self-help," completely agreeing with the following words of Henry David Thoreau: "In the morning I bathe my intellect in the stupendous and cosmogonal philosophy of the Bhagavad Gita in comparison with which our modern world and its literature seem puny and trivial."

If there is one book that has the permanent solution to all the problems that we see in the world and experience in our own lives, it is the Bhagavad Gita. If each person in this world starts following the principles taught in the Bhagavad Gita, most of those issues will never even arise. And, even if we do happen to encounter a problem, we will be so well-prepared that it will have no impact on us. Bold claim? It is. This is, however, a fact.

Following the advice given in this one book alone can keep us happy for the rest of our lives. In fact, we do not even understand what true happiness is; because we have never experienced it. The Bhagavad Gita can guide us in achieving that eternal state of happiness. This one book is enough to cleanse our minds of all negativity and guide us into a paradise of serenity and bliss.

The Bhagavad Gita has all of the answers to all of the questions worth asking that we've had since the beginning of time. Who am I — a body, a mind, a soul? Where have I come from? What exactly is death? What happens after death? Is there a God? Who is God? How does He look like? Why can't I see Him? Is there one God or are there many Gods? Is there a reason for my existence? If so, what is it?

No other book can claim to give answers to humanity's most fundamental questions, such as these.

The Vedas are the world's oldest religious texts. And the Bhagavad Gita is a distillation of the most significant and relevant aspects of the Vedic philosophy. This makes the Bhagavad Gita the world's oldest philosophy. Apart from being the oldest, it is also the most perfect philosophy. It explains how the universe functions, who God is and what is His purpose, and also who we are, and what we are here to do. It also contains the ideal antidote to all the negativity in our lives.

The Bhagavad Gita even depicts how God looks like, and how we can reach Him. Nowhere else do we find a more vivid description of the characteristics of God.

The Bhagavad Gita explains how nature, as a fragment of Krishna, keeps the universe going, what its various forms and traits are, and how we are deceived by the illusions of the material world. It also reveals how the four-fold Yoga system can help us overcome the pains of the material world.

This is the magic of the Bhagavad Gita.

Overall, the Bhagavad Gita is an all-in-one how-to guide for living the most perfect life possible.

Why did the Lord sing the Bhagavad Gita?

This is a common question I get from spiritual seekers:

"Why did Lord Krishna sing the Bhagavad Gita so long after the material world was created? Didn't those who were born before that time need this knowledge?"

This is a good question. And the answer is hidden inside the Bhagavad Gita itself. The Lord reveals in the opening few verses of Chapter 4 of the Bhagavad Gita that the message contained in the Bhagavad Gita was first imparted by Him to the sun-god at the time of the universe's creation and was then passed down in a methodical manner.

This shows that sincere seekers have always had access to this knowledge.

The Vedas explain that each time God creates this material world, the age of the world is divided into four periods, called *Yugas*. These are Satya, Treta, Dvapara, and Kali. The Satya-Yuga is characterized by goodness and religion and lasts 1,728,000 years. In the Treta-Yuga, vice is introduced and continues to rise in the Dvapara-Yuga. These yugas last 1,296,000 and 864,000 years, respectively. In the Kali-Yuga (the age we are living in) the ignorance of religion and prevalence of strife reaches its peak and it lasts 432,000 years.

Therefore, the need for such divine knowledge is the greatest in the Kali-Yuga. The Kali-Yuga began as soon as Krishna left this world to go back to His holy abode, Vaikuntha. But, before He left, He wanted to make sure that His real devotees in this dark age of Kali-Yuga had enough support for spiritual progress. So, He contrived this situation so that He could empower future generations with this much-needed divine information.

Bhagavad Gita — A guide beyond religion

Let's be very clear about one thing. The Bhagavad Gita is *not* a religious book. It's a guidebook for life, a how-to manual. The words 'Hindu' or 'Hinduism' appear nowhere in the Bhagavad Gita, or any Vedic scripture for that matter.

Throughout the Bhagavad Gita, Lord Krishna refers to 'beings' rather than 'Hindus.' This is because this song divine is not intended to be read and acted upon by the adherents of a particular religion. This is intended for all people. It is a medicine for the infected souls of the Kali-Yuga. And there is no religion in medicine.

There were no separate religions in the world when the Lord uttered the Bhagavad Gita to Arjuna. Sanatana Dharma, which means 'eternal religion,' was the common religion of all humanity. Sanatana Dharma is the primordial religion of mankind. No matter how many faiths we construct for our own convenience and ego gratification, the reality remains that Sanatana Dharma will always be our actual religion, and Lord Krishna will always be our true object of worship.

As soon as Arjuna realizes this, he says to the Lord, "You are imperishable and the supreme one to be known; You are the ultimate repository of this universe; You are inexhaustible; You are the protector of Sanatana Dharma; You are the eternal person. This is my opinion." [BG 11.18]

How is this book different?

I have been a student of the Bhagavad Gita for almost two decades. During this time, I also read various books on the subject, including many translations and verse-by-verse commentaries. Even though most of these authors claim to have translated the Sanskrit verses accurately, I always found a few verses whose translations appeared to be affected by the author's preexisting beliefs. This always lowered my interest in the translation and weakened my trust in it.

This book, which you have in your hands, is my attempt to fill that void. I have the highest regard for all of the translators and authors whose works I've read, and I can't deny that I've learned a great deal from them. Also, I make no claim that this is the most 'correct' translation of Gita. However, I have made every effort on my part to ensure that this book contains an accurate translation of each verse, without any bias toward a specific stream of thought or philosophy.

Although I've tried to keep the translations simple, I've also tried to make sure not to do that at the cost of accuracy, essence, or the spirit of the Bhagavad Gita. I have given context due importance while establishing the meaning of each word with the aim of providing correct interpretation. Also, the gaps arising while translating verses from Sanskrit to English have been taken care of to preserve the intended meaning of each verse.

The verses in this translation include brief explanations that should greatly assist the reader in comprehending the meaning of each verse (more on this in the next point). In addition, the explanations at appropriate places — at the beginning, middle, and end of each chapter — should help the reader grasp the teachings of the Bhagavad Gita quite easily. In this revised and updated version of the translation, I have made a few significant changes with the aim of making this translation even easier to read and understand and to make the meaning of each verse absolutely clear to the reader.

A note to the reader (Important)

In this translation, I have added explanations and clarifications in parentheses at appropriate points in the verses to ensure that the reader understands the essence of each verse.

This book seeks to provide not only an authentic translation of the Bhagavad Gita but also to ensure that the reader understands the deeper meaning concealed behind each of its magnificent verses. This is impossible without sufficient contextual assistance. The only other way for me to ensure proper understanding was to avoid the texts in parentheses and instead provide lengthy commentaries on each verse. Commentaries, however, disrupt the flow of the verses and typically cause readers to lose patience. And so, my only option was to use short, easily digestible phrases in parentheses provided in the verses themselves wherever necessary. It would have been an injustice to you — the reader, the seeker — if I had avoided them, and I would have been guilty of offering only half-truths. In any case, I have included such explanations only where they are essential and inevitable. When you begin reading the verses, you will immediately recognize and appreciate the value of such explanations and clarifications.

I have just one more thing to add here. Most readers find the Bhagavad Gita quite easy to comprehend. However, if, for whatever reason, you find it slightly hard to follow at first, my suggestion is not to become discouraged and give up. The Bhagavad Gita is not a light-hearted read; it contains essential life-changing information. A little difficulty in the beginning should not prevent you from seeking the divine wisdom contained in this scripture. Patience and perseverance will undoubtedly benefit you. I promise things will get easier and clearer as you go along, and that it will all be worth it in the end. You will surely become a lot more blissful by the time you finish this book if you keep an open and accepting frame of mind. That is a guarantee.

Now, as I believe I have equipped you with everything you might need beforehand, let us now plunge into the sacred pool of enlightenment known as the Bhagavad Gita.

Chapter 1 - Arjuna's Grief

Dhritarashtra (to Sanjaya):

(1) O Sanjaya, when my sons and the sons of Pandu assembled on the holy plain of Kurukshetra, desiring to fight, what did they actually do?

The Bhagavad Gita begins with King Dhritarashtra, who is blind (both physically and spiritually), asking his charioteer-guide Sanjaya to inform him of the current situation on the holy battlefield of Kurukshetra, where his own sons, the Kauravas, and the sons of his deceased brother, the Pandavas, have gathered to battle for the kingdom of Hastinapur. The first verse of the Bhagavad Gita is Dhritarashtra's only utterance in the holy scripture. The rest of the Bhagavad Gita depicts Sanjaya's observations on the battlefield before the start of the great war of Mahabharata. Dhritarashtra is clearly concerned about the outcome of the great conflict, and thus desires to know what is going on on the battlefield.

Sanjaya (to Dhritarashtra):

(2) Having seen the army of the Pandavas drawn up in battle formation, King Duryodhana approached the teacher (Drona) and spoke the following words.

Duryodhana (to Dronacharya):

(3) O teacher, behold this great army of the sons of Pandu, arranged in battle formation by your talented disciple — the son of Drupada (Dhrishtadyumna).

In a sense, Duryodhana is criticizing Dronacharya for passing on his military knowledge to Dhrishtadyumna, who is now fighting on the opposing side.

(4) Here are mighty heroes, excellent archers, equal in war-skills to Bhima and Arjuna, great warriors like Yuyudhana, Virata and Drupada (the father of Draupadi).

(5) There's Dhrishtaketu, Chekitana, and the valiant King of Kashi, Purujit, Kuntibhoja, and Saibya — the heroes among men.

(6) There's also the mighty Yudhamanyu, the valiant Uttamaujas, the son of Subhadra (Abhimanyu) and the sons of Draupadi — all, verily, commanders of great chariots.

However, uttering these names seems to shake Duryodhana from inside. So he asks Dronacharya to now listen to the names of the mighty warriors who are fighting for his (Duryodhana's) sake.

(7) But, O best of the twice-born (Brahmins), also be appraised of the generals of my army, who are the most prominent amongst ourselves; these I name now for your information.

(8) There's your good self, Bhishma, and Karna, and Krip — the ever-victorious ones; Ashvatthama (Drona's skillful son), Vikarna, and the son of Somadatta, and Jayadratha.

(9) And numerous other heroes are also there, prepared to lay down their lives for my sake, all of them well-equipped with various weapons, and well-skilled in battle.

(10) The strength of our army, well-protected by Bhishma, is unlimited, whereas the strength of their army, defended by Bhima, is limited.

(11) Therefore, all of you, stationed at your respective strategic positions in the different divisions of the army, must protect Bhishma.

We can easily sense a distinct whiff of anxiety in the words of Duryodhana. Drona is already familiar with the make-up of both sides. By reciting the names of the able warriors fighting on his side,

Duryodhana is merely trying to persuade himself that he will surely win this war. He is trying to convince himself that he will be victorious as his side is stronger and these valiant warriors are all equipped with the best weapons. Duryodhana is also demonstrating his egoistic mentality by listing the names of warriors who are "prepared to lay down their lives for my sake," as he puts it.

In an attempt to calm his pounding heart, Duryodhana claims that his side, being headed by Bhishma, the greatest warrior ever, is much stronger than that of the Pandavas, which is led by Bhima who, according to him, is not nearly as capable a leader, boosting Duryodhana's prospects of victory.

Therefore, he asks Dronacharya to make sure that Bhishma receives the full support of him and the other warriors from their respective positions on the battlefield. He knows it is impossible to lose while Bhishma is alive, and so he wants to ensure Bhishma's protection from all sides.

Sanjaya (to Dhritarashtra):

(12) The eldest of the Kuru dynasty, the valiant Grandsire (Bhishma), to raise his (Duryodhana's) joy, then blew his conch, sounding as loud as a lion's roar.

(13) Then suddenly, a chorus of conchs, kettledrums, tabors, trumpets, and horns erupted (from the side of the Kauravas); the sound became deafening.

(14) Then, Madhava (Krishna) and Pandava (Arjuna), seated in their grand chariot yoked with white horses, blew their divine conchs.

(15) Hrishikesha (Krishna) blew His conch named Panchajanya; Dhananjaya (Arjuna) blew his conch named Devadatta; and Vrikodara (Bhima), the performer of terrible deeds, blew the great conch, Paundra.

(16) King Yudhisthira, the son of Kunti, blew his conch Anantavijaya; Nakula and Sahadeva blew their conchs Sughosha and Manipushpaka respectively.

(17) And the King of Kashi — an excellent archer, and Shikhandi — the great warrior; Dhrishtadyumna, and Virata, and the unconquerable Satyaki, ...

(18) ... Drupada, and the sons of Draupadi, and the mighty-armed son of Subhadra (Abhimanyu) — all blew their respective conchs, O Lord of Earth.

(19) That uproarious sound (coming from the side of the Pandavas) reverberated through the sky and the land, and shattered the hearts of the 'clan of Dhritarashtra.'

In the olden days, the blowing of conchs was a way to signal the beginning of a battle. By reading these verses we can understand that, although the sound of conchs of the Kaurava side was tumultuous, it paled in comparison to that of the Pandava side, which has made the hearts of the warriors on the Kaurava side tremble.

(20) Then, O Lord of Earth, beholding the 'clan of Dhritarashtra' arrayed to fight, and the discharge of weapons about to begin, Pandava (Arjuna), whose flag bears the emblem of monkey (Hanuman — the great devotee and assistant of Lord Rama, a previous avatar of Krishna), took up his bow and spoke these words to Hrishikesha (Krishna).

Arjuna (to Lord Krishna):

(21) O Achyuta, please place my chariot between both the armies ...

(22) ... until I survey all of those who are arrayed here desiring to fight, and who will fight with me in this impeding battle; ...

(23) ... for I wish to observe those who have gathered here to fight, wishing to please the evil-minded son of Dhritarashtra (Duryodhana).

Sanjaya (to Dhritarashtra):

(24) O descendant of Bharata, thus addressed by Gudakesha (Arjuna), Hrishikesha (Krishna) drove the best of chariots in the midst of the two armies, ...

(25) ... in front of Bhishma, Drona, and all the rulers of the world, and said, "O Partha (Arjuna), behold all the assembled members of the Kuru dynasty."

(26) There Partha saw, within both armies, fathers, grandfathers, teachers, maternal uncles, brothers, sons, grandsons, and also associates, fathers-in-law, and friends.

(27) Kaunteya (Arjuna), seeing all these kinsmen thus arrayed, became overwhelmed with great compassion, and spoke thus sorrowfully.

Arjuna (to Lord Krishna):

(28) Seeing these kinsmen, O Krishna, arrayed, ready to fight, my limbs are failing, and my mouth has become dry.

(29) Also, my body is trembling, and my hair is standing on end, the Gandiva (Arjuna's famous bow) is slipping from my hand, and also my skin is burning.

(30) I am also unable to stand firmly, and my mind seems to be rambling. I can only see adverse omens, O Keshava.

(31) Besides, I do not see any good in killing my own kinsmen in war. O Krishna, I have desire for neither victory, nor kingdom, nor pleasure.

(32) O Govinda, of what avail to us is dominion; of what avail is pleasure, or even life?

(33) The very ones for whom we desire kingdom, enjoyment and pleasure stand here in battle, having renounced life and wealth — ...

(34) ... teachers, fathers, sons, and also grandfathers, maternal uncles, fathers-in-law, grandsons, brothers-in-law, and other kinsmen.

(35) I do not wish to kill them, O Madhusudana, even though I may be killed by them, not even for the dominion over the three worlds, what to speak of the earth.

(36) What pleasure can we gain from killing the sons of Dhritarashtra, O Janardana? Sin alone with come upon us by slaying these felons.

(37) Therefore, it is not proper on our part to kill the sons of Dhritarashtra, our own relatives. O Madhava, how can we be happy by killing our own kinsmen?

(38) Although they, with their hearts eclipsed by greed, see no evil in destruction of families, and in enmity with friends, ...

(39) ... why should not we, who can see the evil in annihilation of families, know to turn away from this act of sin, O Janardana?

(40) With the destruction of the family, the age-old religious rites of the family are vanquished; and with the destruction of spiritual traditions, sin overpowers the entire family.

(41) With the prevalence of irreligion, O Krishna, the women of the family become corrupt; and with the contamination of the women, O Varshneya, comes intermingling of castes.

(42) Intermingling of castes (not recommended in the Vedas) verily leads the destroyers of the family and the family itself to hell. The ancestors of such families, being denied the oblations of rice-balls and water (prescribed in the Vedas for their peaceful stay in the heavens), are degraded.

(43) By such evil deeds of the destroyers of the family, which causes intermixing of castes, the age-old religious rites of the caste and the clan are destroyed.

(44) We have heard, O Janardana, that it is inevitable that the ones, the religious rites in whose families have been destroyed, dwell in hell.

(45) Alas! What a pity that we have decided to commit a great sin by being prepared to kill our own kinsmen, driven by greed for the pleasures of a mere kingdom.

(46) If the sons of Dhritarashtra, with weapons in hand, kill me in battle, non-resisting and unarmed, that would be better for me.

Sanjaya (to Dhritarashtra):

(47) Arjuna, having thus spoken on the battlefield, his mind distressed with grief, casting aside his bow along with arrows, sat down on the seat of the chariot.

We can see how compassion for his kinsmen overpowers Arjuna's mind. Arjuna, who is counted among the ablest and the bravest warriors of his times, finds himself weakened by sympathy for his friends, relatives, and well-wishers. He can only see bad omens everywhere and is even willing to die rather than fight against and kill his loved ones — even his cousins, the Kauravas, who have done terrible injustices to him and his brothers.

We humans spend our entire lives in a state of tension and bewilderment, never bothering to try to find a permanent solution to such issues. But, for the ones who are willing to look, the solution lies in the coming chapters.

Chapter 2 - An Introduction to Yoga

The second chapter of the Bhagavad Gita deals with the Yoga of transcendental knowledge. It can also be viewed as a summary of the main contents of the upcoming chapters. Yoga is the science of attaining oneness with the Supreme God. One who strives to attain such oneness is a Yogi. In this chapter, Lord Krishna provides an introduction to the various concepts of Yoga — Jnana (right knowledge), Karma (right action), Dhyana (right meditation), and Bhakti (right devotion). He also informs us about our genuine nature and introduces us to our true identity. He also explains what our true purpose in life is. This chapter also contains a brief overview of the most significant mental attributes for seekers to cultivate and avoid. All this makes this a very important chapter from a spiritual seeker's perspective.

Let's now dive into the content of this chapter.

Sanjaya (to Dhritarashtra):

(1) To him who was thus overwhelmed with compassion (Arjuna), having eyes filled with tears, lamenting, Madhusudana (Krishna) spoke these words.

Lord Krishna (to Arjuna):

(2) O Arjuna, in this perilous condition, from where has this impure despondency come upon you, suitable only for unenlightened people, which brings dishonor, and does not lead to heaven?

(3) Do not yield to this impotence, O Partha; it does not befit you. Forsake this petty weakness of the heart, O Parantapa. Arise!

Arjuna (to Lord Krishna):

(4) O Madhusudana, O slayer of enemies, how can I, in combat, fight with arrows against Bhishma and Drona, who are worthy of worship?

(5) It would be better for us to live in this world by begging than to live by slaying my most noble mentors. But, by killing the superiors, surely the wealth and the desired objects that we would enjoy in this world would be tainted with blood.

(6) We do not even know which would be better — that we shall win conquering them or that they shall conquer us. Standing before us are the sons of Dhritarashtra, after killing whom we certainly shall not wish to live.

(7) My mind is overpowered by weak pity and is confused about my duty. I implore You to tell me for certain which is the best path for me. Now I am Your disciple. Please instruct me, who has taken refuge in You.

(8) I just cannot find anything that can, even after attaining a prosperous and unrivaled kingdom on earth, or even supremacy over the gods, drive away this sorrow that is burning my senses.

This is the sign of a true devotee. In times of crisis and confusion, a true devotee of the Lord surrenders *completely* to Him, demonstrating complete trust in his Master. He knows that only He can provide him with the best solution to his problems. This type of submission is not cowardly; rather, it is made in the understanding of the Supreme, and is thus absolutely pure.

Sanjaya (to Dhritarashtra):

(9) Having spoken thus to Hrishikesha (Krishna), Gudakesha-Parantapa (Arjuna), said to Govinda (Krishna), "I will not fight," and verily fell silent.

(10) O descendant of Bharata, to the one who was lamenting in the midst of the two armies (Arjuna), Hrishikesha, as if smiling, spoke these words.

Lord Krishna (to Arjuna):

(11) While you speak words of wisdom, you are grieving for those who are not to be grieved for. The wise mourn neither for the departed (dead) nor for the non-departed (living).

(12) But never indeed, I, at any time, did not exist, nor you, nor all these rulers of men; nor verily, will any of us ever cease to exist hereafter.

(13) As boyhood, youth and old age are for the embodied (the soul) in this body, similar is the attainment of another body; this being so, a wise man is never bewildered seeing such changes.

(14) O Kaunteya, the contacts of senses with the objects, producing the ideas of heat and cold, pleasure and pain, have a beginning and an end, and are non-permanent. Endure them, O descendant of Bharata.

(15) Verily, that man whom these (sensory perceptions) do not afflict, O best among men, the firm man who remains steady in sorrow and happiness — he is alone considered eligible for immortality (liberation).

(16) The unreal (the body) has no existence; the real (the soul) has no nonexistence. Verily, the ultimate truth about both of these is realized by the seers of the truth (the realized sages).

(17) But know that to be indestructible by which all this (the entire body) is pervaded. No one can bring about the destruction of the imperishable (the soul).

(18) These perishable bodies are said to be of the embodied (the soul) — the eternal, the indestructible, the immeasurable. Therefore, fight, O descendant of Bharata.

(19) One who considers this (the soul) as the slayer and one who considers it as the slain, neither of them is in knowledge. It slays not, nor it is slain.

(20) It never takes birth, nor it ever dies; it neither comes into being, nor it ever ceases to be. It is unborn, eternal, changeless, and primeval. It is not slain when the body is slain.

(21) O Partha, how and whom can a person who knows it to be indestructible, eternal, unborn, and changeless, kill or cause to be killed?

(22) Just as a person, casting off worn-out clothes, puts on other new ones, in the same way, the embodied (the soul), relinquishing decayed bodies, verily accepts other new ones.

(23) Weapons cannot cut it, fire cannot burn it, water cannot moisten it, and wind cannot dry it.

(24) It cannot be cut; it cannot be burned, cannot be moistened, and certainly cannot be dried. It is everlasting, all-pervading, undisturbed, immovable, and changeless.

(25) It is said that it is invisible, it is inconceivable, and it is immutable. Therefore, knowing this to be such, you ought not to grieve.

(26) If, however, you think that it takes birth continuously and dies continuously, even then you, O Mahabaho, should not grieve for it; ...

(27) ... for one who has taken birth, death is a certainty, and for the dead, birth is a certainty. Therefore, you ought not to lament over that which is inevitable.

(28) All beings are unmanifest in their beginning (before birth), manifest in their interim state (while living in this world), and certainly unmanifest again after death, O descendant of Bharata. So, what is there to grieve about then?

(29) Someone visualizes it (the soul) as a wonder; another, similarly indeed, speak of it as a wonder; and similarly, another hears of it as a wonder; and another, indeed, even after hearing about it, does not understand it.

(30) O descendant of Bharata, that which dwells in the bodies of everyone (the soul) can never be killed. Therefore, you ought not grieve for all these created beings.

In these words, Krishna reveals to Arjuna the biggest secret about our real nature. He says that we are not our bodies, but are eternal souls. We have always existed and will always exist. We assume new bodily forms each time we take birth on this planet. However, our eternal nature remains unaffected. And since there is no real existence of death, there should be no need for us to worry about our own death or the deaths of our loved ones. We are immortal spirit souls, and this is our true identity.

Krishna continues to give His divine instructions to Arjuna:

(31) Even, indeed, considering your specific duty (as a Kshatriya), you should not waver; for there is nothing better for a Kshatriya than a righteous war.

(32) Happy indeed are the Kshatriyas, O Partha, to whom such opportunities to battle come of themselves, opening for them the doors to heavens.

(33) If, however, you decline to perform your duty to fight this righteous war, then having abandoned your duty and glory, you will incur sin.

(34) People will forever speak of your disgrace; and for one who has been honored, dishonor is worse than death.

(35) The great commanders who have thought highly of you will think that you have withdrawn from the battle out of fear, and will look down upon you.

(36) Also, your enemies will use many words not worthy of being spoken while maligning your might. What could be more painful than that?

(37) Either being slain, you will attain heaven, or by conquering, you will enjoy the earth. Therefore, get up Kaunteya, determined to fight.

In the olden days, one's responsibilities were decided by the cultural rules. According to the Vedas, society was split into four classes in ancient times. These were Brahmins, Kshatriyas, Vaishyas, and Shudras.

Brahmins were society's religious leaders. Kshatriyas ruled and managed the state and protected its people from enemies and other threats. Vaishyas were merchants and farmers. And Shudras were the laborers that served the other classes.

Individuals in each of these classes had to adhere to their assigned responsibilities. For example, Arjuna was a Kshatriya. When he saw his loved ones standing on the opposite side in the great war of Mahabharata, he lost his composure out of compassion for them and refused to fight. However, a Kshatriya's mandated duty was to fight for righteousness, and a Kshatriya with integrity could not refuse to fight in a battle, even if it meant inevitable death. Since Arjuna was perplexed and had forgotten his duty, Lord Krishna sang His eternal divine song to him to educate him about spiritual truths and thus help him regain his calm and sobriety.

Lord Krishna explains here that spiritual advancement is only possible for those who religiously engage in their prescribed duties. Avoiding one's responsibilities is a surefire way to spiritual degeneration. Renunciation is recommended only for fully realized souls, not seekers.

So, it is clear that one should do his best to fulfill one's responsibilities. Even though our society is no longer divided into any such classes, we all have our chosen responsibilities to fulfill. And we need to make sure we perform them to the best of our abilities.

Krishna then goes on to emphasize how important it is to carry out one's responsibilities effectively *without wishing for any particular outcomes*. He says:

(38) Make happiness and sorrow, gain and loss, victory and defeat the same; then, fight for the sake of fighting. By so doing, you will not incur sin.

(39) This knowledge has been imparted to you through the analysis of concepts. But now, listen to this wisdom concerning Yoga, endowed with which, O Partha, you shall be free from the bondage of Karma (material action).

(40) Here (in this path of Yoga), there is no loss of effort (toward liberation), nor is there any harm. Even a little of this knowledge protects one from the great fear (the fear of falling into the vicious cycle of birth and death again).

(41) Here, O beloved child of the Kurus, there is a single-pointed determination; whereas the thoughts of the irresolute are many-branched (distracted) indeed, and are unending (full of endless doubts).

(42) Men of limited intelligence utter, being attracted toward them, all these flowery words of the Vedas, O Partha, saying "There is nothing else."

(43) Being full of desires, they utter flowery words (of the Vedas), which recommend various activities for the attainment of heavens, favorable birth, and power.

(44) Single-pointed determination (to pursue Yoga) and meditation (on the Lord) cannot be established in those who are too attached to material pleasures and opulence, and whose minds are thus bewildered.

(45) The Vedas mainly deal with the subject of the three modes of material nature (purity, passion, and darkness). O Arjuna, rise above these three modes and the pairs of opposites (pain-pleasure, profit-loss, and so on), ever-established in pure spiritual existence, free from the ideas of acquisition and preservation (of material wealth), and be established in the self (the knowledge of being a soul).

(46) To the Brahman (wise Yogi) established in knowledge, all the Vedas have so much use as has a small reservoir of water when there is flood all around.

The Vedas are the world's oldest religious scriptures. These massive volumes of religious teachings include a wealth of material and spiritual information. Those who are not spiritually inclined, however, are drawn to the sections of the Vedas that discuss various religious sacrifices that can help one obtain all the material prosperity and pleasure one desires. But one can only enjoy material joys for as long as one is alive in this world. Thereafter, being too attached to the satisfaction of his senses, he falls down spiritually and finds himself in the unending spiral of material births and deaths.

These fleeting joys should never be pursued as a goal. Instead, we should strive to be free from the three modes of material nature — purity, passion, and darkness (all of which are explained by Krishna in the later chapters), and to always be steady in mind. Knowledge of the soul and the Supreme Soul (God) is sufficient knowledge for us to fulfill our objective in life, which is to attain liberation from the cycle of birth and death and live in the companionship of the Lord.

Krishna goes on to say:

(47) Your right is indeed to perform dutiful actions, but not to the rewards. Never consider yourself as the creator of the rewards of actions, and there must never be an attachment to inaction.

(48) Perform your dutiful actions, O Dhananjaya, being steadfast in Yoga, abandoning all material attachments, and remaining steady in both success and failure. Such equanimity is called Yoga.

(49) Action (performed with attachment to its results) is far inferior to the Yoga of wisdom, O Dhananjaya. Seek refuge in wisdom. Miserable are those who work for rewards.

(50) One who is established in wisdom rids himself of the effects of both virtue and vice even in this material world. Therefore, devote yourself to Yoga, the skill of action.

(51) The masters of the mind, established in wisdom, having abandoned rewards produced from actions, and thus freed from the bondage of births, attain the state beyond evils (by reaching the holy abode of God).

Thus, Lord Krishna explains to Arjuna the essence of Karma Yoga, which is engaging in one's prescribed duties with no desire for favorable results. This often seems counterintuitive to many seekers. Why in the world should one work without any expectations of getting favorable results?

Since childhood, we've been taught to act with the end in mind. A third of the self-help books in a bookstore claim to teach the best way to achieve one's goal. Whatever the activity is — small or significant — it must have a goal or outcome that serves as an incentive to carry it out. And then there's Krishna, oddly telling us to forget about the outcome and just keep performing our duties. How can this be logical?

We must understand that Krishna never suggests ignoring the outcome. He suggests we *stop worrying* about the outcome. In other words, He advises we should act diligently, but that should be the extent of our concern. To pass the test, a student must prepare diligently. But his action is the only thing he should be concerned about. There should be no need to be worried once he has taken action and given it his all. He has no control over the outcome.

Concerning ourselves with the consequences of our actions ties us to this world. If you are worried about the consequences of your actions, it shows that you believe *you* are in control.

On the other hand, right action though does not guarantee immediate positive outcomes, does guarantee a positive move toward freedom, which is a much better outcome than anything we might hope for.

Krishna continues imparting the enlightening divine wisdom to Arjuna, and through him to all of us. He says:

(52) When your intellect crosses the darkness of delusion, then you shall become indifferent to all that is yet to be heard and all that has already been heard (all kinds of past and future material experiences of the senses).

(53) When your mind, though bewildered by all that it has heard, stands fixed and steady in the soul, then you will attain Yoga (self-realization), that arises from wisdom.

In short, Krishna emphasizes the significance of being wise by always remaining conscious of the fact that we are not our bodies, but are eternal souls. This material life is a temporary playground for us to attain liberation from births and deaths and to reach our true home — the home of Krishna. This should be our only true goal in life. While living on this planet, we should engage ourselves in performing our duties wholeheartedly, without worrying about their outcomes. The only outcome we should worry about is whether or not Krishna would love us for this. As a result, we will always remain steady in mind, without being disturbed either by the objects of sense pleasure or by the external situations of joy and sorrow. This is the highest form of wisdom.

Arjuna (to Lord Krishna):

(54) O Keshava, what is the description of one who possesses steady wisdom and is merged in transcendence? How does a man of steady wisdom speak, how does he sit, how does he walk?

Lord Krishna (to Arjuna):

(55) O Partha, when one completely gives up all desires of the mind, and is satisfied in oneself through the realization of being a soul, then he is considered to be established in steady wisdom.

(56) One who is not shaken up by adversity, or hankers after pleasures in times of prosperity, is free from attachments, fear, and anger, is called a sage of steady mind.

(57) One who is free from attachment everywhere, neither joyous in obtaining anything good, nor hateful on meeting anything bad, is established in firm knowledge.

(58) Also, when he, like a tortoise withdrawing its limbs (within the shell), withdraws his senses from the sense-objects, then his wisdom becomes steady.

(59) The sense-objects, turning away from the one who abstains from them, leave behind the taste (longing for them in his mind). But one who beholds the Supreme (in his mind, through pure devotion) is freed even from the taste.

(60) The turbulent senses, O Kaunteya, do forcibly carry away the consciousness of one of discriminating intellect, even while he is striving diligently to control those senses.

(61) Restraining all his senses, fully controlled, one should concentrate on Me. One whose senses are under control has a steady consciousness.

(62) While brooding on sense-objects, a person develops attachment to them; such attachment produces lust; from lust arises anger (because of non-satisfaction); ...

(63) ... from anger comes delusion (due to the resulting mental disturbances); from delusion arises loss of memory (about the true identity of oneself); from loss of memory arises loss of intelligence (sense of discrimination between the real and the unreal); and from loss of intelligence, one perishes (falls down in his spiritual progress).

(64) However, a person of restraint roaming among objects of sense pleasure, but having his senses in control, being free from both attraction and repulsion, attains peace.

(65) In that blissful state, all pains are destroyed; for the intelligence of an even-minded person soon becomes well established.

(66) There can be no wisdom for the unsteady, nor can the unsteady have the ability for meditation (on the Supreme); and for one without meditation, there is no peace. How can there be happiness for one without peace?

(67) One's power of discrimination is driven away when the mind focuses on the wandering senses, just as wind sweeps away a boat off course on the water.

(68) Therefore, O Mahabaho, his intelligence is steady whose senses are absolutely restrained from sense-objects.

(69) The self-controlled person keeps awake during the time which is the night to all beings; that time during which all beings keep awake is the night for the conscious sage.

(70) That person attains peace into whom all desires enter, just like the waters enter the ocean, which remains ever undisturbed even while constantly getting filled; not the one who savors such desires.

(71) That person attains peace who, giving up all desires, moves about without longing, devoid of the ideas of 'I' (identifying himself with his mortal body) and 'mine' (material ownership).

(72) O Partha, this is the state of being established in the Brahman (the Supreme Lord); being established in this state, one never gets deluded. Becoming thus situated even at the moment of death, one attains oneness with the Supreme.

Thus, Lord Krishna, in these wonderful words of wisdom, enlightens all seekers about the path to attain Him. A crucial requirement to become liberated is to give up all desires of sense satisfaction and attachment to the material objects, as such desires and attachments never allow us to concentrate on our divine goal. We must also strive to achieve mental stability and tranquility by realizing that emotions arise from sense perceptions, and thus we need not be affected by emotions of any kind. The Lord reveals that the best way for us to attain freedom from senses and emotions is to keep our focus on Him. When one falls in love with Krishna, he never has to struggle for freedom from his senses and the constant flow of the seemingly positive and negative emotions.

Because of his conscious nature, resulting from regular practice of this knowledge, a true Yogi (one who strives for oneness with the Supreme Lord) has a radically different perception of everything from that of an ordinary mortal. This is the state we should strive for, as it clears the path to the kingdom of Krishna.

Chapter 3 - The Yoga of Action

In the third chapter of the Bhagavad Gita, Lord Krishna explains, in much detail, the concept of Karma Yoga to Arjuna.

Arjuna, perplexed by all the knowledge about the different forms of Yoga provided to him by Krishna, implores the Lord to dissolve his confusion.

Arjuna (to Lord Krishna):

(1) O Janardana, if knowledge is considered by You to be superior to action (performed with a desire for favorable results), why then do You, O Keshava, want to engage me in this ghastly activity?

(2) With these apparently conflicting statements, You are confusing my intelligence. Therefore, please tell me decisively that *one* way by which I may achieve the highest good.

Lord Krishna (to Arjuna):

(3) O sinless one, I have already spoken of the two kinds of faiths in this world — Jnana Yoga (or Sankhya Yoga — Yoga of knowledge) for the wise, and Karma Yoga (Yoga of action) for the Yogis (of action).

(4) A person cannot attain freedom from action by merely abstaining from work, nor by mere renunciation can he attain perfection (of human existence).

(5) Verily, no one can ever remain, even for a moment, without performing action; for everyone is compelled to act helplessly by the attributes born of (one has acquired from) material nature.

(6) One who, restraining the organs of action, sits thinking of sense-objects in his mind, he, of a deluded mind, is called a hypocrite.

(7) But, one who, disciplining the senses by the mind, O Arjuna, engages the organs of action in Karma Yoga (performing dutiful action without expectation of favorable results, and dedicating the action and its results to the Supreme Lord), without attachment (to results), excels.

(8) Perform your prescribed duties, for action is certainly superior to inaction. Also, even the maintenance of your body is not possible through inaction.

(9) Actions, other than those performed as an offering to God, result in bondage in this world.

Therefore, O Kaunteya, perform your duties, devoid of attachment, only for Him.

In this way, Lord Krishna again clarifies the concept of Karma Yoga (Yoga of action) to Arjuna. He says that inaction is not desirable. So one should definitely not shy away from engaging oneself in his prescribed duties. But one's actions should be devoid of any sense-cravings and attachments to desired results, and should be performed as an offering to the Almighty God. He continues:

(10) At the beginning of creation, the divine creator (Brahma), having made mankind along with sacrifice, said, "By this (sacrifice) shall you prosper. Let this be the milch cow (a mythological cow capable of fulfilling all of one's desires) of your desires."

(11) You nourish the gods with this (sacrifice); may the gods in return nourish you with this (the rewards of the sacrifices one makes). By nourishing one another, you will attain the supreme benediction (association of the Supreme God).

(12) The gods, being satisfied by the performance of sacrifices, will indeed provide you with the objects you desire. But, he who enjoys what has been given by the gods without offering the same in return to them, is certainly a thief.

(13) Sages who eat the remnants of the sacrifices (food that is offered first as a sacrifice to gods) are freed from all sins; but the sinful ones who prepare food for their own sense-satisfaction incur sin.

(14) From food grains arise creatures; from rain come food grains; from sacrifices come rains; sacrifices are born of Karma (right action).

(15) Know that actions come from Brahma (the Supreme Creator), and Brahma is manifested from the Imperishable (the Supreme God). Consequently, the all-pervading vibration (of God) is inherently present in sacrifice.

(16) One who does not follow here the wheel (of sacrifice) thus set rotating (by God), and who thus lives a sinful life, settled in the senses, lives in vain, O Partha.

(17) But one who rejoices in the self (the knowledge of being a soul) alone, and is satisfied with the self (not hankering after material objects), has no material duty.

(18) For him there is neither any meaning here in performance of actions, nor any meaning in non-performance; nor is he dependent on any other being for any purpose.

(19) Therefore, keep performing your prescribed duties without attachment (to their results); for by performing work without attachment a person attains the Supreme.

So, what is Karma Yoga? Simply put, Karma Yoga is nothing but performance of one's duties without any desire for specific results, but rather as a sacrificial offering to Lord Krishna, the Supreme Person. The Lord explains that one should never work for the sake of obtaining material benefits. The only purpose of work for us should be to offer it to our Master. Working for our own selfish motives is sinful, as that is not the aim with which the Lord has sent us to this planet.

This material human life is a very rare and significant opportunity for us to fulfill our goal of liberation from this material and illusory world. Therefore, if we use it to work for sense-gratification, without offering the results of work (in any form, for example, food) to the Lord, or at the very least, to the various forms of the Lord (the demigods), we commit a grave spiritual offense. We should act only out of duty.

Lord Krishna continues His teachings:

(20) Janaka (a pious king and the father-in-law of Lord Rama, a previous incarnation of Krishna) and others like him verily attained perfection through right action alone. Therefore, also for the sake of protecting the masses in general, you ought to act.

(21) Whatever a superior person does, the common men also do. Whatever he upholds as the standard, the world pursues.

(22) O Partha, there is no work prescribed for Me in the three worlds, nor do I have anything to obtain — yet, I engage Myself in action.

(23) For if I ever fail to engage Myself continually in action, being vigilant, O Partha, all men will imitate My way in every respect.

(24) If I do not perform actions, all these worlds would be ruined. I would be the cause of confusion of prescribed duties amongst castes, and would thus ruin all beings.

(25) As the ignorant perform actions with attachment (to rewards), O descendant of Bharata, the wise must do so without attachment, wishing for the welfare of the masses.

(26) A wise man should never disturb the minds of the ignorant persons who are attached to the prospective rewards of actions. Rather, himself working with devotion, he should engage them in their duties.

Hence, a wise person (one who is in knowledge of the soul and the Supreme Soul) should work without expecting favorable outcomes, not only for his own sake, but also to serve as a leader to those who have not had the opportunity yet to develop their intellect spiritually, and are thus living in the darkness of ignorance.

The Blessed Lord further says:

(27) While all actions are actually carried out by the attributes of material nature, one whose intelligence is deluded by ego (resulting from identifying oneself with the body) thinks, "I am the doer."

(28) But he who knows the truth about the different modes of material nature and how they work, O Mahabaho, and knows that these attributes exist in both the senses and the sense-objects, never becomes attached to them.

(29) Those who are ignorant, being deluded by the attributes born out of material nature, become attached to the activities of the attributes (actions one is subconsciously made to perform by the attributes one acquires from material nature). A man of perfect knowledge should not unsettle those lacking such knowledge.

(30) Surrendering all kinds of activities unto Me, with your mind centered on the self (the soul), free from expectations (desires for favorable results), ego (sense of ownership), and feverish anxiety (worries about failure), fight.

(31) Those who constantly follow these instructions of Mine (about Karma Yoga) faithfully, without fault-finding, become free from the bondage of material actions.

(32) But those who disregard this teaching of Mine and do not practice it, bereft of all knowledge, devoid of understanding, know them to be doomed (in their spiritual endeavors).

(33) Even a man of knowledge acts according to his own nature; for all beings follow the nature (attributes they acquire from the three modes of material nature). What can artificial suppression do?

(34) Attachment and aversion toward sense-objects generate from the senses. One should not come under their influence; for they are his enemies (as they do not allow one to remain even-minded and progress spiritually).

(35) Better is discharging one's own duty, even if it lacks quality, than another's duty performed well. Death in the course of performing one's own duty is better; performing another's duty is fraught with fear (of being spiritually degraded).

As Krishna explains, all activities are the products of the natural attributes that we are given when we take birth in this material world. There are three classes of such attributes which Krishna elaborates on later. However, here it is critical for us to understand that we must remain unattached to activities (and their potential rewards), and perform them simply as a duty. In fact, we should be able to do this so naturally that we won't have to fight our instincts. Suppressing wants is a sign that we *have* them, which is not recommended. We must be free of material cravings to the point where they will never touch us and we will never have to suppress them. Understanding this can help us go forward in our spiritual journey, while failing to appreciate it might be detrimental to our spiritual efforts.

Arjuna (to Lord Krishna):

(36) Then, O Varshneya, by what is one impelled to sinful acts, even against his will, as if compelled by force?

Lord Krishna (to Arjuna):

(37) This desire, this anger (resulting from desire), born of the material mode of passion, is highly devouring and highly sinful. Know this as the enemy here.

(38) As fire is obscured by smoke, as a mirror by dust, and as the embryo is enveloped by the womb, so is this (one's intelligence) covered by that (material desire).

(39) Wisdom is covered by the constant enemy of the wise in the form of desire, O Kaunteya, as if by the fire that is never satisfied.

(40) The senses, the mind, and the intellect are said to be the seats of it (desire). Through all these, it deludes the embodied soul by eclipsing its wisdom.

(41) Therefore, O most superior among the descendants of Bharata, after first controlling the senses, slay this sinful destroyer of knowledge and wisdom (material desire).

(42) The senses are said to be superior (to the physical body); the mind is superior to the senses; and the intelligence is superior to the mind; but the one superior even to the intelligence is he (the spirit soul).

(43) Knowing the self (the soul) thus, as superior to the intelligence, restraining the self (from getting deluded) by the self (the knowledge of being a soul), annihilate this enemy, in the form of desire, which is hard to conquer, O Mahabaho.

Lord Krishna thus concludes this chapter by describing one of the biggest roadblocks to spiritual advancement that may delude our intelligence and lead us down the path of darkness and unconsciousness. That roadblock is the material desire of varying degrees. It is the desire that drives us to do things for the sake of material gain rather than out of devotion to our master, Lord Krishna. This results in nothing but sin. Hence, to become a Yogi, it is critical for us to get rid of material desires. The only way to do so is to replace it with the desire for Lord Krishna's association, which is the highest and the purest form of desire.

Chapter 4 - The Yoga of Knowledge

After teaching the science of Karma Yoga — achieving oneness with the Supreme through right action — in the previous chapter, Lord Krishna outlines the process of achieving the same goal via Jnana Yoga (Yoga of knowledge) in this chapter. Action without knowledge proves to be counterproductive. Hence, to progress spiritually, right knowledge is critical. Knowledge (Jnana) can give Action (Karma) a whole new meaning. And so, the presence of knowledge is essential for action to be effective. None can be without the other, or they falter.

Lord Krishna (to Arjuna):

(1) I taught this imperishable Yoga (the science of getting one with God) to Vivasvan (the sun-god); Vivasvan taught it to Manu (the father of humankind); and Manu passed it on to Ikshvaku (the founder of the solar dynasty in which the Lord appeared as Rama).

(2) This knowledge was thus handed down through orderly succession, and was received by the royal sages in that way. But, by long lapse of time here, the great science of Yoga was lost, O Parantapa.

(3) Verily, that same ancient science of Yoga is today told to you by Me, as you are My devotee as well as My friend. This knowledge is a supreme secret.

Krishna lays out the history of spiritual knowledge in these lines, leaving no room for speculation or doubt. It all makes sense, especially when we consider all the other information found in the Bhagavad Gita and the other Vedic texts. When all of this information is considered together, it becomes clear how the eternal divine knowledge has been transmitted down through the ages. Although the Bhagavad Gita was sung by Lord Krishna five thousand years ago, the knowledge contained in it was disseminated by Him as soon as He created the universe. That is why it is the purest and the most original form of knowledge.

Not only does the Lord explain the ancient significance of this knowledge here, but He also mentions how this complicated knowledge can be understood in its true essence. One needs to be a devotee and a friend of Krishna to understand this intricate and confidential science of Yoga if one wants to become His associate and live in His divine abode for eternity.

Arjuna (to Lord Krishna):

(4) Your birth was later; Vivasvan (the sun-god) was born earlier. How am I to understand this that You instructed thus (to Vivasvan) in the beginning of creation?

Arjuna's question to the Lord is essentially a layman's query. Krishna is no ordinary human, as Arjuna is well aware. However, he is unable to think clearly because of his bewilderment, and consequently is asking the Lord such questions. Of course, the kind Lord purposefully created such a situation in order to rekindle this divine knowledge for the benefit of future generations of mankind. Arjuna's incomprehension has caused him to regard Krishna as an ordinary being.

Lord Krishna (to Arjuna):

(5) O Arjuna! Many births of Mine have passed, and also yours. I know them all, but you not, O Parantapa.

(6) Although I am unborn, am of imperishable nature, and am the Lord of all beings, yet, subjugating My own divine nature, I incarnate by My own nature (in Krishna's own way — not like a human takes birth normally).

(7) Whenever there is a decline in religion (virtue), and a predominant rise in irreligion (vice), O descendant of Bharata — I manifest Myself (as an avatar).

(8) For the protection of the pious and for the annihilation of the wicked, and thus to reestablish righteousness, I appear in every age.

(9) One who truly understands the divine nature of My appearance and activities does not, upon leaving the body, take birth again; he comes to Me, O Arjuna.

(10) Being freed from attachment, fear, and anger, being fully absorbed in Me, taking complete shelter in Me, and sanctified by the penance of gaining knowledge, many have attained My nature (by becoming one with Krishna).

(11) In whatever way men approach Me, I reward them accordingly. All humans, in all ways, follow My path, O Partha.

(12) Desiring the fruits of their actions here, they (human beings) worship the demigods by making sacrifices; for material success is achieved quickly through result-oriented work in this mortal world.

(13) The four-fold caste system has been created by Me according to the different modes of nature and the related actions. But although I am its creator, you should know Me as non-doer and immutable (as Krishna Himself is not a part of that system).

(14) Action does not taint Me, nor have I desire for the rewards of actions. One who knows Me thus does not become entangled by actions.

(15) Work was performed even by the ancient seekers of liberation in this knowledge. Therefore, you should perform your dutiful actions, as did the ancients of the olden times.

In this way, the Lord presents a brief overview of His divine character. He remembers all the births of all living beings, which is only possible for the Supreme God. He is unborn, being outside of the confines of time and space that bind us. Being the eternal person, He never dies. He arrives at opportune times in the material world in varied forms. Only those who, by the practice of Yoga, establish themselves into perfect knowledge of the soul and the Supreme Soul (the all-knowing God), and thus become His pure devotees, can cross this material ocean and reach the Supreme.

The Lord thereafter clarifies that, though He is the Supreme Doer, His actions have no effect on His nature (unlike in the case of material beings), and so He effectively remains a non-doer. So, one should understand the Lord in this way, and be engaged in one's duties in such knowledge.

Krishna continues:

(16) What is action? What is inaction? Even the wise are confused regarding this. I will explain to you the true meaning of action, knowing which you shall be liberated from evil (the spiral of births and deaths in the material world).

(17) For, verily, action has to be understood, and forbidden action has to be understood, and inaction has to be understood. The true nature of action is imponderable.

(18) One who recognizes inaction in action and action in inaction is wise among men; for he is transcendental, though engaged in performing actions.

(19) Whose endeavors are devoid of desires and purposes (Karma Yoga), and whose actions are burned in the fire of knowledge (Jnana Yoga), he the sages call wise.

(20) Abandoning all attachment to the fruits of work, ever content and independent (of material wants), though engaged in activities, he, verily, performs no binding action.

(21) Performing mere bodily actions, without any expectations of return, with his mind and intellect under control, having abandoned all sense of ownership, such a man incurs no sin.

(22) Content with what comes to him of its own accord, having transcended the dualities (gain-loss, rich-poor, etc.), being free from envy, and being steady in both success and failure, he, though performing actions, is not bound (by their reactions).

(23) Of a man who is free from attachment, of the liberated man, whose mind is situated in knowledge, and who acts as sacrifice (devoting the work and its results to Krishna), all actions dissolve fully (thereby not creating any effects on his future lives).

No discussion on true knowledge can be considered complete without a discussion on what constitutes desired action. Both of these, along with the other elements of Yoga, are needed for one to attain the purpose of one's life by reaching the all-attractive Krishna. Hence, the Lord again provides a brief explanation of Karma Yoga, as was discussed in the previous chapter.

He further says:

(24) The offering is Brahman (of divine nature), the clarified butter (poured in the sacrificial fire) is Brahman, the sacrificial fire itself is Brahman, the oblation (sacrificed in the fire) is Brahman. Brahman (God) is verily reached by him, all of whose activities are concentrated on the attainment of Brahman.

(25) Some other Yogis offer sacrifices to the demigods alone; some others offer 'sacrifice' itself as sacrifice in the fire of the Brahman (the Supreme God).

(26) Some offer hearing and the other senses as sacrifice in the fires of restraint (thus vowing to engage the senses only in pure spiritual endeavors); others sacrifice sound and the other objects of the senses in the fires of the senses (vowing never to indulge in them).

(27) Others offer the activities of all the senses or the activities of the life-breath into the fire of the Yoga of self-control, kindled by knowledge.

(28) Again, others offer sacrifice of wealth, sacrifice through the practice of penances, sacrifice through the practice of Yoga, or sacrifice through study and acquisition of knowledge, and ascetics accept strict vows as sacrifice.

(29) Others offer as sacrifice, the movement of the outgoing breath into the incoming, and others the incoming breath into the outgoing, controlling the flow of the outgoing and the incoming breaths by the practice of *Pranayama* (controlled breathing).

(30) Others, regulating their diet, offer pure outgoing breath into the air as a sacrifice. All these are knowers of sacrifice, whose sins are destroyed by their sacrificial activities.

(31) Only the eaters of the nectar-like remnants of sacrifices go to the Eternal Brahman (God). Even this world is not for the non-performer of sacrifices, what to say of the other (the divine world), O best of the Kurus?

(32) Thus, various kinds of sacrifices are spread through the mouth of Brahmans (as mentioned in the Vedas); know them all to be born of action. Thus knowing, you shall become liberated.

(33) O Parantapa, the sacrifice of knowledge (the practice of acquisition of divine knowledge) is superior to the mere sacrifice of material objects. All acts of sacrifice, in their entirety, culminate in knowledge, O Partha.

The Lord thus describes the meaning and significance of sacrifices in one's spiritual pursuits. The sacrifices that Krishna is talking about here are not some religious obligations to be carried out halfheartedly to please the gods and have them fulfill one's material wants. These are sacrifices made with complete awareness of the true identity of the self (as a soul) and the Supreme, with the sole purpose of purifying one's mind and thus making oneself fit for liberation from this world.

Sacrifices are of several types. The Lord gives a few examples for our understanding. One can, for example, forego mundane entertainment in favor of studying holy scriptures; one can meditate on the Lord with an absolutely purified mind free of lustful thoughts; one can relinquish eating impure food that cannot be offered to the Lord; or one can take a vow to live an ascetic life free of sexual desires. Whatever the sacrifice, it must be offered to the Supreme Brahman (Lord Krishna) with knowledge of His actual nature and awareness of His presence in all components of nature. Of course, the more kinds of sacrifices one may practice, the better it will be for his spiritual progress.

The Blessed Lord further explains:

(34) Know that through surrender, through inquiry, and through service, the wise sages who have seen the truth, will impart that knowledge to you, ...

(35) ... knowing which, O Pandava, you will never again come under such delusion; and by which you will see all beings in yourself (being of the same nature as oneself), and also in Me (as a part of the Supreme).

(36) Even if you are the biggest sinner among all sinners, by the boat of knowledge, you will certainly be able to cross all oceans of sin.

(37) As a blazing fire reduces firewood to ashes, O Arjuna, similarly the fire of knowledge reduces all reactions of material actions to ashes.

(38) Verily, there is nothing so purifying here (in this material world) as knowledge. One who has become perfected in Yoga finds it within himself in due course of time.

(39) A man full of faith, who is dedicated to the attainment of that transcendental knowledge, and has subdued the senses, attains it; and having attained the knowledge, he, without delay, attains the supreme peace (of self-realization).

(40) However, one who is ignorant and faithless, and has a doubting mind (have baseless doubts about the truth in the teachings given in the scriptures or imparted by the realized souls), perishes (in his spiritual endeavors). For a person of doubting mind, there is neither this world (the material realm), nor the next (the spiritual realm), nor bliss (that emanates from Godhead).

(41) Actions do not bind one who has renounced the rewards of work by the practice of Yoga (getting one with the Supreme), whose doubts have been annihilated by knowledge, and who is poised in the knowledge of the self, O Dhananjaya.

(42) Therefore, with the sword of knowledge, cut asunder this doubt about the self (about being a soul), born in your heart out of ignorance. Take refuge in Yoga of knowledge. Arise, O descendant of Bharata!

Lord Krishna thus explains the importance of the knowledge revealed by Him in the Bhagavad Gita and expanded upon in the other Vedic scriptures. One should ideally seek out this knowledge from a realized sage. And once one has fully grasped this knowledge, there is nothing that can prevent him from entering Krishna's divine kingdom. This knowledge frees one from the shackles of the effects of one's Karma, which may bind him to this material world and lead to another miserable life here. Thus, one should never doubt the authority of the divine scriptures and the authoritative knowledge given therein.

In the previous chapter, Krishna talked about Karma (right action). In this chapter, He takes us one step closer to liberation by explaining Jnana (right knowledge). In this way, the Lord inspires Arjuna (and, through him, all of us) to give up all material wants and perform our duties without any expectations (Karma Yoga), in full knowledge of the self (the soul) and Krishna (the Supreme).

Chapter 5 - True Renunciation

In Chapter 3, Lord Krishna says, "But one who rejoices in the self alone, and is satisfied with the self, has no material duty." However, throughout Chapters 3 and 4, He advocates the performance of one's prescribed duties, being established in knowledge, without attachment to results. Arjuna, though in a better frame of mind than before, is unable to understand the different contexts in which the Lord has given the two seemingly opposing instructions. Arjuna is confused, and so he requests the Lord to erase his perplexity.

Arjuna (to Lord Krishna):

(1) O Krishna, You praise renunciation of actions, but also Yoga (of action — Karma Yoga). Please tell me conclusively that *one* which is better of these two.

Lord Krishna (to Arjuna):

(2) Renunciation of action and Karma Yoga (Yoga of action, or performance of action without expectations and with devotion to the Supreme Lord), both lead to liberation. But, of the two, Karma Yoga is superior to renunciation of action.

(3) One who neither hates nor craves (the rewards of his activities) is to be known to be constantly renounced; for, being free from pairs of opposites, O Mahabaho, he is easily freed from bondage (of material work).

(4) Children (the ignorant), not the wise, speak of Sankhya (Yoga of knowledge, also called Jnana Yoga) as being different from Yoga (of action — Karma Yoga). One who is fully established in even one of these two receives the rewards of both.

(5) That state that is attained by the Sankhyins (those who practice Yoga of knowledge) is also attained by the Yogis (of action). One who sees Sankhya and Karma as one sees the truth.

(6) But renunciation is hard to attain, O Mahabaho, without Yoga (of action). By the practice of Yoga, a sage quickly attains the Supreme.

(7) Engaged in Yoga, a pure soul, being self-controlled, having control over his senses, and seeing his own self as the self of all beings (being aware that all beings are pure spirit souls), though performing actions, is never tainted (by the effects of Karma).

(8) The knower of the truth, engaged in self-consciousness, thinks, "I certainly do not do anything," even while seeing, hearing, touching, smelling, eating, moving, sleeping, breathing, ...

(9) ... speaking, releasing, receiving, opening and closing the eyes — being well aware that only his material senses work amid the sense-objects.

(10) Dedicating his actions unto the Brahman (God), he who acts renouncing attachment (to the results of his actions) is not tainted by sin, just as the lotus leaf remains unaffected by water.

(11) The Yogis (of action), renouncing attachment, perform actions with the body, mind, intellect, and senses, only for the purification of the self.

(12) Thus engaged, renouncing the rewards of actions, being steadfast, one attains peace; whereas one who is not thus engaged, ruled by desire and attached to the rewards, becomes entangled (in the effects of Karma).

(13) Mentally renouncing all activities, and keeping the senses in control, the embodied one (the soul) resides blissfully in the city of nine gates (the material body), neither working nor making others (the senses) work.

(14) Neither God creates, for the people of the world, agency (the illusion of being doers of actions), nor does He cause them to do activities, nor does He entangle them in the rewards of their actions. But it is material nature that acts.

(15) The Lord does not accept anyone's sin, and not even virtue (as taking account of one's vice and virtue is the function of Karma and not of God). Knowledge is eclipsed by ignorance, thereby beings are deluded.

(16) But whose ignorance is destroyed by the knowledge of the self (being the soul), the knowledge, like the sun, reveals to them the Supreme.

(17) Those whose intelligence is immersed in That (the Supreme God), soul is one with That, faith is given to That, who have taken That as the supreme goal, their sins being cleansed through knowledge, reach the state of no return (liberation from material births and deaths).

(18) The wise sages, endowed with knowledge and humility, look with an equal eye upon a Brahmin (a learned man of the highest class), a cow, an elephant, a dog, and even an outcast (the different grades of lower creatures).

(19) Birth has been conquered (by attainment of liberation), even here (in this world), by those whose minds are established in equanimity. Brahman (the Supreme God) is flawless and balanced indeed; therefore they (the wise) are established in the Brahman.

(20) The knower of the Brahman, being ever situated in the Brahman, steady-minded, and free from delusion, neither rejoices upon obtaining something pleasant, nor grieves upon obtaining something unpleasant.

(21) One whose mind is not attached to external objects of sense pleasure, finds joy within the self. Engaging the self (the mind) in meditation on the Brahman, he enjoys eternal bliss.

(22) The pleasure coming from contacts (of material senses with material objects) only causes misery, for they have a beginning and an end. O Kaunteya, the wise do not delight in them.

(23) One who is able, while still here, before giving up the body, to withstand the impulses created out of desire and anger, is a Yogi (one who endeavors to become one with God); he is a happy man.

(24) One who is happy within, who rejoices within, who is illuminated within (is established in perfect knowledge), that Yogi, being absorbed in the Brahman (the Supreme God), attains oneness with the Brahman.

(25) Those sages whose sins have been annihilated, who are free from doubts, whose senses are in control, who contribute to the welfare of all beings, achieve liberation in the Brahman.

(26) Those ascetics who are free from material desires and anger, who are self-controlled and self-realized (having knowledge of the soul), are soon liberated in the Brahman.

(27) Shutting out all external contacts (with sense-objects), fixing his vision between the two eyebrows, and making even the inward and outward breaths moving within the nostrils, ...

(28) ... controlling the senses, mind, and intelligence, the sage aiming at liberation, free from desire, fear, and anger, verily attains everlasting liberation.

(29) One who knows Me as the ultimate enjoyer of all sacrifices and austerities, the Supreme Lord of all worlds, and the friend of all beings, attains peace (through liberation).

Lord Krishna recommends that we approach Karma Yoga and Jnana Yoga equally. It is just as crucial to know oneself and the Supreme as it is to engage in pure action.

Also, what is important for us to realize is that we must give up a few things as soon as possible: a desire for objects that provide temporary and impure material pleasure to the senses, a desire for the rewards of actions, thinking of ourselves as bodies (and thus nurturing false ego and considering ourselves as the controller), and succumbing to negative mental attributes like anger. This, not the abdication of responsibility, is true renunciation.

We must keep our sights set on our ultimate aim of transcending the material world, always maintaining a steady image of Krishna in our minds, seeing Him everywhere and in everything. As a result, our material lives shall be filled with peace and happiness, and we shall be ready to enter our next lives in Krishna's divine abode.

Chapter 6 - The Yoga of Meditation

Chapter 6 of the Bhagavad Gita contains the best advice on mind-management that cannot even be found in the bestselling self-help books available. Mind is the most important tool provided to us by Lord Krishna. Most of us, however, do not use it in the ideal manner, instead stuffing it with all kinds of needless and impure thoughts and emotions that hamper spiritual advancement. Lord Krishna, in this chapter, provides us with the best way to use our minds to reach Him.

Lord Krishna (to Arjuna):

(1) One who performs his dutiful acts without taking shelter of (depending on) the rewards of actions is a renunciate and a Yogi; not he who does not light the fire (of knowledge) and is actionless.

(2) O Pandava, know that what they (the scriptures) call renunciation is the same as Yoga (getting one with the Supreme); for without renouncing thoughts (of rewards and sense gratification), one cannot become a Yogi.

(3) For a sage who desires his elevation in Yoga, action (Karma Yoga) is said to be the means; and for the one who has become elevated in Yoga, inaction (mental steadiness) is said to be the means.

(4) One is said to be elevated in Yoga when he becomes unattached to sense-objects and actions, having renounced all impure thoughts.

(5) Let man lift his self (the mind) by the self (the knowledge of being a soul), not degrade his self (into ignorance and thereafter destruction); for the self (the mind) is the friend of oneself, and it (the deluded mind) is also the enemy.

(6) For him whose self (the knowledge of being a soul) has conquered the self (the mind), the self (mind) is the best friend of the self (soul); but to the unconquered self (the deluded mind), its enemy, the self (the soul), remains an enemy.

(7) One who has subdued his self (the mind), and is thus blissful, is completely established in the Supreme Self (God) in cold and heat, pleasure and pain, and honor and dishonor.

(8) A Yogi who is satisfied in knowledge and realization, who is steady, who has subdued his senses, to whom soil, stone and gold are the same, is said to be self-situated.

(9) One is considered spiritually advanced when he regards the good-hearted ones, friends, foes, relatives, neutrals, mediators, the hateful, the virtuous and the sinners — all with an equal mind (knowing them all to be spirit souls).

In this way, Lord Krishna explains the importance of the mind for spiritual progress. One needs to keep it controlled, always established in the supreme knowledge of the soul and the Supreme Soul, completely divorced from sense desires and rewards of activities, and always in equanimity. In the coming verses, He further describes the most recommended method of restraining the mind and keeping it focused.

(10) Free from hope (expectations of favorable results) and desires for material possessions, living alone in a secluded place (ideal for engaging oneself in meditation on God), with a controlled mind and body, a Yogi should constantly keep his mind focused (on God).

(11) His seat, situated in a clean place, should be firm, neither too high nor too low, and covered first with *kusha*-grass, then with deer or tiger skin, and finally with a cloth.

(12) Sitting there, with a single-pointed mind, controlling the activities of the mind and the senses, he should practice Yoga (Dhyana Yoga or Raja Yoga — Yoga of meditation) for the purification of the soul (making it fit for liberation).

(13) Holding his body, neck and head erect and still, being steady, gazing at the tip of his nose, without looking around, ...

(14) ... being serene in mind, devoid of fear, firm in the vow of celibacy (devoid of sexual desires), subduing the mind, the Yogi should sit, meditating on Me as the Supreme Goal.

(15) Ever concentrating the mind thus, the self-balanced Yogi attains peace, abiding in Me, which culminates into *nirvana* (liberation, also called *moksha*).

(16) But, O Arjuna, Yoga (of meditation) is not for one who eats too much, nor for one who does not eat at all, also not for one who sleeps too much, nor also for one who always keeps awake.

(17) For one who is moderate in his habits of eating and recreation, moderate in efforts in work, and moderate in sleep and wakefulness, Yoga (of meditation) becomes the destroyer of pain.

(18) When the perfectly controlled mind is established in the soul, free from all desires for sense-objects, one is said to be united (with Krishna).

(19) A lamp in a windless spot does not flicker. This simile may be used to describe a Yogi, who has controlled his mind by the practice of meditation on the self (the soul).

(20) When the mind, restrained through the practice of Yoga of meditation, attains quietude, and thus the self (ego, identifying oneself with the body) sees itself as the self (the soul), and finds contentment in the self (being an individual soul — a part of the Supreme Soul); ...

(21) ... when the Yogi experiences immeasurable bliss, which can be grasped by the intelligence and which transcends the senses, being thus established, he does not move from the reality (of being a soul).

(22) The state (of self-realization), once obtained, is considered by the Yogi as the gain beyond all other gains, established in which he remains unshaken even in the mightiest sorrow.

(23) That stage is known as Yoga — the stage of freedom from pain. This Yoga should be practiced resolutely, with a steady and stout mind.

(24) Abandoning all desires born out of material purposes, in full, and controlling all senses from all sides with the mind, ...

(25) ... he (the Yogi) should, slowly and gradually, become situated in tranquility, by his firm intelligence, his mind being established in the self (the soul as his true identity), free from any other thoughts.

(26) Wherever the flickering and restless mind wanders, he must withdraw it from all those distractions, and bring it back under the control of the self alone.

(27) The Yogi whose mind has attained perfect calm (through the practice of Dhyana Yoga), who has controlled the passions, who is free from sin, and has become one with the Brahman (God), attains the highest state of bliss.

(28) The Yogi, engaging the self (the mind) in this way, free from impure thoughts, easily attains the supreme bliss of contact with the Brahman.

(29) With the mind absorbed in Yoga (of meditation), he sees the Supreme Self (God) in all beings, and also sees all beings in the Supreme Self; indeed, he sees the same everywhere.

(30) One who sees Me everywhere, and sees everything in Me, never loses Me, nor is he ever lost to Me.

(31) Such a Yogi stays always in Me, who, being established in unity (with Krishna) in all circumstances of life, worships Me as the one dwelling in all beings.

(32) He who, realizing the sameness of the souls, O Arjuna, sees equality all around, in both joy and sorrow, is the best kind of Yogi.

Meditation is generally thought of as a beneficial technique for calming the mind, relieving stress, and improving attention. However, meditation is not merely a mundane mental practice to be carried out with these objectives in mind. Meditation is a God-given boon for people like us who are always engaged in trivial material activities, seeking sense-pleasures, to make us aware of our true nature and the nature of the Supreme God, and to reach Him by connecting with Him on a regular basis.

Lord Krishna suggests that we meditate on our newfound understanding of our true selves. Also, we should meditate on Him with devotion and a mind that is free of all material pollution. Such a practice of meditation with the intention of uniting with the Supreme Lord is called Raja Yoga or Dhyana Yoga. Only through regulating and purifying our daily routines will we be able to achieve this. As a result of such practice, we should eventually arrive at a position where we view everyone as a soul, with God in them and them in God. This will bring us happiness and tranquility in this world, and God's companionship in the next.

However, this is easier said than done due to the restless nature of the human mind. And Arjuna has the same problem with Krishna's instructions.

Arjuna (to Lord Krishna):

(33) O Madhusudana, due to restlessness (of the mind), I do not see how this Yoga of equanimity, that has been explained by You, can have enduring continuity.

(34) Verily, the mind is restless, turbulent, powerful, and stubborn, O Krishna; I consider it as difficult to control as the wind.

Lord Krishna (to Arjuna):

(35) O Mahabaho, undoubtedly, the mind is difficult to control and restless; but, by practice (of the Yoga of meditation) and dispassion, O Kaunteya, it can be controlled.

(36) Yoga (union with God), in My opinion, is difficult to attain for one with an uncontrolled self (mind); but he who, being self-controlled, strives, can certainly obtain it with proper means (by the practice of the Yoga of meditation).

For the resolute, controlling the mind is no big issue. He remains established in perfect knowledge, and therefore takes care of his thoughts, which makes him a devout Yogi.

Arjuna (to Lord Krishna):

(37) O Krishna, what happens to one who is unsuccessful in Yoga — who had taken to Yoga with faith, but was unable to control himself, as his mind wandered away from Yoga?

(38) Fallen from both (material as well as spiritual progress), does he not, O Mighty-armed, without refuge, and deluded in the path to the Brahman (God), perish like a riven cloud?

(39) Please dispel completely this doubt of mine, O Krishna; for none other than You can possibly dispel this doubt.

Because the human mind is restless by nature, it is quite easy for a Yogi to stray from his path by becoming distracted by sense-objects or other impurities found in this material world. Arjuna is concerned about this, and he asks Krishna for help.

Lord Krishna (to Arjuna):

(40) O Partha, neither here (in this material world) nor hereafter (in the spiritual world) is there destruction for him (a failed Yogi); verily, My son, no one who does good ever meets misfortune.

(41) The fallen Yogi, after entering the worlds of the virtuous (heavens), and living there for several years, is again born (on Earth) in the home of the righteous and the rich.

(42) Or, (depending on his previous spiritual progress) he is born in the family of the wise Yogis; verily, such a birth is hard to obtain in this world.

(43) There, he recovers the wisdom acquired in the previous body, and strives more than before for spiritual perfection, O beloved child of the Kurus.

(44) By virtue of the former practice (of Yoga), he is carried forward in spite of himself (having no such inclination initially). Even one who merely wishes to know Yoga theoretically stands farther advanced than a follower of the ritualistic scriptural principles (described in the Vedas).

(45) And, by striving diligently, the reborn fallen Yogi, purified of sins, attaining perfection after the efforts of many lives, thereby attains the supreme goal (Krishna's association).

We can see the fair and merciful nature of the Supreme Lord Krishna here. He knows that it is difficult for a seeker to remain focused in this tempting material world full of attractions and distractions. Therefore, He ensures that a fallen seeker has a favorable birth in his next material life, allowing him to pursue liberation with much more determination and focus.

(46) A Yogi (one who constantly meditates on the Lord) is superior to the ascetic (who does not pursue the Lord), is also superior to the men of theoretical knowledge, and is also superior to the men of action (motivated by rewards). Therefore, be a Yogi, O Arjuna.

(47) And of all types of Yogis, the one who, being full of faith, merging himself in Me, worships Me — he I regard as the most devout.

Lord Krishna thus declares that one who meditates on Him is a superior seeker to one who relies on theoretical knowledge or works with the aim of getting favorable results. In Chapter 12, He goes into greater detail about this.

Chapter 7 - The Supreme and His Nature

After describing the various methods to attain Him, Lord Krishna, in this chapter, reveals to Arjuna the greatest secrets about His own nature, known only to His true devotees, who are ever established in knowledge and constantly endeavor for His association.

Lord Krishna (to Arjuna):

(1) Hear, O Partha, how by practicing Yoga (of meditation), having the mind absorbed in Me, and taking refuge in Me, you can know Me completely, beyond any doubt.

(2) I shall declare to you in full this knowledge, combined with practical realization, which being known, nothing more remains to be known here.

(3) Among thousands of men, perhaps one strives for perfection; and among those who diligently strive for perfection, perhaps one knows Me in essence.

Krishna thus declares to Arjuna that the knowledge of Him is the peak of all knowledge. However, only the best of seekers get to know Him as He truly is.

(4) Earth, water, fire, air, space, mind, intelligence, and ego — these eight separate elements constitute My material nature.

(5) This is My inferior nature. Different from it, do understand, O Mahabaho, My superior nature — the very life-element (soul) by which this material world is upheld.

(6) Know that these (Krishna's two natures) comprise the womb (source) of everything. Understand that I am the creator as well as the annihilator of the entire universe.

(7) There is nothing whatsoever superior to Me, O Dhananjaya. All things (beings and objects) are strung in Me, as a row of gems on a thread.

(8) O Kaunteya, I am the taste of water; I am the light of the moon and the sun; I am the syllable "Om" in all the Vedas; the sound in space; and virility in men.

(9) I am the sweet fragrance in the earth; and I am the luminescence in the fire; the life in all beings; and the penance in the ascetics.

(10) Know Me to be the eternal seed of all beings, O Partha. I am the intelligence of the intelligent; I am the splendor of the splendid.

(11) And I am the strength of the strong, devoid of desire and attachment. However, I am the passionate desire (for self-realization) in beings, not contrary to the duties of human existence (striving for perfection), O best among the descendants of Bharata.

(12) Know all manifestations of existence indeed, be they pure, passionate or dark, to have emanated from Me. They are in Me (as Krishna contains the whole creation); yet, I (Krishna's all-powerful, all-encompassing divine Self) am not in them.

(13) The entire world, deluded by these three modes (purity, passion, and darkness) of material nature, does not understand Me to be beyond these, and as inexhaustible.

(14) Indeed, this divine illusion of Mine, consisting of the modes of material nature, is difficult to cross over. Only those who take refuge in Me can cross over this illusion.

(15) The miscreants, the deluded fools, the lowest among men, whose wisdom is stolen by material illusion, who follow the path of demonic beings, do not seek shelter in Me.

(16) O best among the descendants of Bharata, four kinds of virtuous men worship Me — the distressed, the seekers of knowledge, the seekers of wealth, and the wise (those who know Krishna's real nature).

(17) Of them, the wise, ever engaged in devotion, is the special one; for I am very dear to the wise, and he is dear to Me.

(18) All of these (the four kinds of worshipers) are indeed noble, but the wise I consider as My own Self; for, being mentally steadfast, he is settled in Me as the highest goal.

(19) After numerous births, the wise man attains Me, realizing Me to be everything. Such a great soul is very hard to find.

Krishna is the Supreme Being. He may assume material forms in this world, but that does not make Him an ordinary human being. He is the source of everything and also the destroyer. He is the most superior one and exists in all elements of the universe — both tangible and intangible.

The unfortunate ignorant souls, deluded by material nature, cannot understand Him. To know Him, one must seek refuge in Him by entirely surrendering to Him, and perceive Him as the highest goal.

(20) Those whose intelligence has been stolen away by the various kinds of material desires move to worshipping other gods (the demigods), following the particular demigod's respective injunctions of worship, according to their (the deluded souls') own natures.

(21) Whatsoever form (demigod) a devotee desires to worship with faith, I make that very faith of his unflinching (not forcing him to worship Krishna directly).

(22) Endowed with that faith, he engages in worship of that form (demigod), and from that worship gains fulfillment of his desires; however, in reality, these satisfactions of desires are indeed arranged by Me alone.

(23) The rewards gained by men of little intelligence (the worshipers of the demigods) are limited (perishable). The worshipers of the demigods go to the abodes of the respective demigods; whereas My devotees come to Me (Krishna's abode — *Vaikuntha*).

Clearly stating the hierarchy of the spiritual world, Lord Krishna declares that He is the Supreme God. Demigods have been created by Him to fulfill the material desires of the deluded souls. However, the source of the powers of the demigods is Lord Krishna Himself. Worshipping demigods can provide temporary material pleasures only. But to experience eternal bliss, a seeker must worship Krishna directly.

(24) The unintelligent ones think of Me as the unmanifest who has become manifest (assuming human-like body), not perceiving My higher nature — imperishable and supreme.

(25) I am not manifest to all, veiled by My material (human-like) form. The deluded world knows Me not — the Unborn, the Imperishable.

(26) O Arjuna, I know all the beings of the past, the present, and the future; but Me no one knows.

(27) O descendant of Bharata! O Parantapa! All beings are immersed into delusion (forgetting the spiritual truths about themselves and God) at birth, bewildered by the dualities arising from desire (likes) and aversion (dislikes).

(28) But men of virtuous deeds (undertaken over several lifetimes), whose sins have been fully negated (by such virtuous deeds), being freed from the delusion of duality (likes and dislikes), worship Me, remaining steadfast.

(29) Those who strive for liberation from old age and death, taking refuge in Me, know that Brahman (Krishna Himself), everything about the self (soul — *Adhyatma*), and about actions (*Karma*).

(30) Those who perceive Me in the physical manifestations (material beings — *Adhibhuta*), in the godly beings (demigods — *Adhidaiva)*, and also in sacrifices (as the beneficiary — *Adhiyajna*), with their minds thus engaged, can perceive Me even at the time of death.

Lord Krishna is present everywhere. However, we forget Him, and we forget our own true nature as well, as soon as we take birth in this material world and come into contact with material nature. Such contact deludes our minds into the illusion of opposites — our likes and dislikes, for example. However, going through several lifetimes, we progress, regaining that lost wisdom and devoting ourselves to Krishna, thereby returning where we truly belong in the end — the divine abode of our Master.

Chapter 8 - The Imperishable Supreme

At the beginning of Chapter 8, Arjuna, befuddled by so many concepts introduced to him at the end of the previous chapter, requests Lord Krishna to clarify their meanings, which the compassionate Lord gladly does. By studying this chapter, we, the students of God's divine song, can get an even deeper insight into the true nature of the Lord and the best ways to approach Him.

Arjuna (to Lord Krishna):

(1) O Purushuttama! What is *Brahman* (the all-pervading Supreme Soul, God)? What is *Adhyatma* (the individual soul pervading all beings)? What is *Karma* (material action)? What is *Adhibhuta* (the perishable consciousness existing in material beings including humans)? And what is *Adhidaiva* (the limited divine consciousness existing in the demigods)?

(2) O Madhusudana! What is *Adhiyajna* (the supreme beneficiary of all sacrifices, God), and how *Adhiyajna* dwells in the material body? And how, at the time of death, can You be known to the self-disciplined ones?

Lord Krishna (to Arjuna):

(3) *Brahman* is the indestructible and Supreme One (God); His essential nature is *Adhyatma* (the individual soul); action causing material beings to take birth (by binding them to the material world) is known as *Karma*.

(4) O best of the souls! *Adhibhuta* is the perishable physical manifestation (body); *Adhidaiva* is the divine consciousness of the Supreme Person (dwelling in the demigods); and I, the Spirit within the body of every being (being the object of all sacrifices and devotion) am *Adhiyajna*.

(5) And whoever, in the last moments of his life, while quitting the body, goes forth remembering Me alone, attains My Being (by gaining oneness with Krishna). There is no doubt about this.

(6) Whatever state of being one remembers in the end, while giving up his body, O Kaunteya, that very state he will attain, because of his persistent thought of it.

(7) Therefore, always remember Me, and fight. Dedicating your mind and intelligence unto Me alone, you will attain Me without doubt.

(8) He who, with a mind not deviating to other things, is engaged in Abhyasa Yoga (regular practice of meditation on the Supreme God), meditating on the effulgent Supreme Person, O Partha, reaches Him by constantly thinking of Him.

(9) One who meditates upon the Omniscient, the most Ancient, the Controller, smaller than the atom, the maintainer of all, of inconceivable form, luminous like the sun, beyond the darkness (ignorance), ...

(10) ... at the time of death, with an undeviating mind, engaged fully in devotion by the power of Yoga (regular practice of meditation), fixing his life breath between the eyebrows, certainly attains the Supreme Effulgent Person (God).

(11) That which the knowers of the Vedas declare as the imperishable, That into which the ascetics and renunciates enter, That desiring which they practice celibacy — the method of attaining That Goal I shall explain to you in brief.

(12) Closing all the gates (of the senses), confining the mind in the heart, fixing the life-breath in the head, and thus engaging in the practice of Yoga (meditation on the Supreme), ...

(13) ... chanting the divine syllable "Om" — the holy word of the Brahman — and remembering Me, he who quits the body, certainly attains the Supreme Goal (Krishna's association).

(14) I am easily attained by that Yogi who regularly and constantly remembers Me, without ever deviating to other things, O Partha.

(15) Having attained Me, the great souls, having reached the highest perfection, never take birth again in the temporary place full of miseries (the material world).

(16) O Arjuna, all material worlds up to the world of Brahma (the most senior of all created gods), are subject to repeated births. But upon reaching Me, O Kaunteya, there is no rebirth (in any of the material worlds).

In these verses, the Supreme Lord Krishna elegantly expresses the divine truths, knowing which one can understand the goal of one's life and then seek to accomplish it. Krishna repeatedly stresses upon meditating on Him with single-pointed devotion, without getting distracted by any material attractions.

After accomplishing this, one's thoughts become grounded in the Lord. Quitting this body with such a mindset certainly opens for the Yogi the door to God's divine abode, reaching where a soul never needs to return to this "temporary place full of miseries." Loving devotion to the Lord surely paves the way for the liberation of the devotee.

(17) Those who know the day of Brahma (Lord's creator form), which runs for a thousand ages, and the night, which also runs for a thousand ages, they truly know 'day' and 'night.'

(18) At the coming of day, all beings become manifest from the unmanifest state; and at the coming of night, they dissolve verily into what is called the unmanifest.

(19) Being born again and again, O Partha, the same throng of beings are annihilated (into the unmanifest state), helplessly, at the coming of night; and they again manifest at the coming of day.

This is how the universe actually works. When compared to the age of creation, our lifetime, no matter how long or short it appears to us, is insignificant.

(20) But there exists another Unmanifested nature (Krishna's divine home), transcendental to that unmanifested nature (where soul's go after annihilation of body before returning to the mortal world), which is eternal, and is not annihilated when the manifested nature (mortal world) is annihilated.

(21) That which is said to be the Unmanifested nature, the imperishable, is thus known as the highest goal, reaching which one never returns (to this mundane material world). That is My supreme abode.

In the last two verses, the Lord has mentioned three levels of planets, the lowest among which are the mortal worlds — such as the Earth — full of pains and suffering. Higher than that are the planets where the souls go to dwell after leaving the material bodies, depending on the collective status of their Karma. If their actions were virtuous, they go to the heavenly planets, and if evil, they go to the hellish planets. There they enjoy or suffer punishment respectively, and once the effects of their Karma have been negated, they are returned to the mortal world.

However, the really pious souls, being the true devotees of the Lord, who become perfected in Yoga while living their material lives, go directly to God's realm — the highest planet of all — to enjoy divine bliss forever, to never return to the lower planets.

(22) The Transcendental Person (God), O Partha, can be attained by unalloyed devotion to Him alone, within whom all beings dwell, and by whom all that exists (beings and objects) is pervaded.

(23) I shall now explain to you, O best among the descendants of Bharata, the times at which the Yogis (those who strive for liberation) depart from this world to never come back, as also to come back.

(24) Fire, light, daytime, the bright fortnight, the six months of the northern solstice — following this path (passing away in these times), those who know the Brahman go to the Brahman.

(25) Smoke, nighttime, also the dark fortnight, and the six months of the southern solstice; the Yogi following this path (who passes away in these times), having attained the moon light (a heavenly illusion), returns (to the material world).

(26) The paths of light and darkness — these two ways of passing from this world — are verily considered to be eternal; by one (the path of light) a man goes not to return; by the other (the path of darkness) he returns again.

(27) Knowing these two paths, O Partha, a Yogi is never deluded. Therefore, at all times, remain steadfast in Yoga, O Arjuna.

(28) The Yogi who knows this goes beyond all declarations in the Vedas regarding the rewards springing from righteous deeds, performing sacrifices, undergoing penances, or doing charity. He reaches the supreme and the original state (by attaining liberation).

Unalloyed devotion to Lord Krishna is the key to liberation, and you can see that the Lord is doing His best to make it absolutely clear to us, the seekers. The Vedas contain details about several rituals which can easily provide us with all the pleasure we may desire, in this world, or in the heavenly world. But those rituals can never free us. We would always be susceptible to pain and misery, as we would be forced to return to this world of suffering every time we die.

Reaching God is the only solution. And the only way to do that is to worship Him, the blissful Lord Krishna, not superficially, but by gaining knowledge of Him, by constantly meditating on Him, by always working for Him, and finally by developing true transcendental love for Him.

This will ensure we leave our bodies at the best time, in the best manner, in the desired mental state, assuring our deliverance and eternal stay with Him.

Chapter 9 - The Royal Secret

Most of us wish to achieve some big goal in life, as advised by our well-meaning elders and friends. The self-help literature too focuses on techniques that can help the readers achieve their 'bigger' goals in life. It's all good, except for one problem. These goals are all material in nature, meaning they are temporary goals, achieving which can only provide the achiever with temporary joy. Our lives are very short when compared to the summation of all the time gone in the past and yet to come in the future. And that means, no matter how grand our goals may seem to us, they are effectively very small.

In this chapter, Lord Krishna reveals the big secret about our actual goal in this material life, after achieving which nothing else remains to be achieved for us. And He also explains *how* we can achieve that divine goal. Read on to know more.

Lord Krishna (to Arjuna):

(1) To you, who does not carp, I shall now impart this most confidential knowledge and realization, knowing which you shall be liberated from evil (miseries of this material existence).

(2) This sovereign education, the sovereign secret, the supreme purifier, directly realizable through undertaking of one's righteous duties, practicing which provides one with joy, is eternal.

(3) The ones not having faith in their eternal duty (to strive for self-realization and liberation), O Parantapa, not attaining Me, return to the material world, on the path of death.

(4) I, in My unmanifested form, pervade this entire universe; all beings exist in Me, but I (Krishna's all-powerful Self) am not situated in them.

(5) Nor do, in reality, the created beings exist in Me. Behold My divine opulence with which I maintain all beings. My Self, being the source of all beings, is not a part of these beings (as the Creator is always separate from the created).

(6) Understand that just as the mighty wind, moving everywhere, rests always in the sky (but is separate from the sky), similarly all created beings are situated in Me (but are separate from Krishna).

(7) All beings, O Kaunteya, at the end of the cosmic cycle, enter into My nature; at the beginning of the next cycle, I create them again.

(8) Entering into the nature of My Self, I create all these manifestations (created beings) again and again, all helplessly subjected to the forces of material nature.

(9) These activities, however, O Dhananjaya, do not bind Me — the one being neutrally situated, unattached to these activities.

(10) Under My supervision, this material nature produces everything moving and unmoving (beings and objects). For this reason, O Kaunteya, the world revolves (in cycles of Brahma's days and nights).

(11) The ignorant fools deride Me when I assume the human form, not knowing My supreme nature as the Great Lord of all beings.

(12) Of vain hopes (of happiness), of vain (misdirected) actions, of vain (material) knowledge, devoid of sense, they verily become possessed of the delusive nature of devils and demons.

(13) But the great souls, O Partha, taking shelter of My divine nature, engage in My devotion without deviation of mind, knowing Me to be the imperishable source of all beings.

(14) Always chanting My glories, striving with determination, bowing before Me (in adoration), they are always engaged in worshipping Me with devotion.

(15) Others, who engage in sacrifice of knowledge (Jnana Yoga) also worship Me, as one, as diverse, as many, as the universal one facing all sides (as the one who encompasses all elements of the entire creation).

(16) I am the rite, I am the sacrifice, I am the oblation to the ancestors, I am the healing herb, I am the holy chant. I am also the clarified butter (used in the sacrificial fire), I am the sacrificial fire, I am the oblation (put into the fire).

(17) I am the father of this entire universe, the mother, the support, and the grandsire (the oldest ancestor). I am the object of knowledge, the purifier, and the cosmic syllable *om,* the Rig, the Sama, and the Yajur Vedas, ...

(18) ... the goal, the maintainer, the Lord, the witness, the abode, the refuge, the dearest friend, the origin, the annihilation, the foundation, the treasure-house, and the imperishable seed.

(19) O Arjuna, I give heat, and I withhold and pour down the rain; I am immortality, and also death; I am both the truth (the spirit) and the false (the physical body).

(20) The knowers of the three Vedas, and the drinkers of the *soma* juice (the immortality-providing drink), purified from sin, worship Me by making sacrifices, praying for an entry into heavens. Attaining thus the holy (heavenly) planet of Indra (the king of heavenly demigods), they enjoy godly pleasures.

(21) Having enjoyed in the vast heavenly planets, they (virtuous men), once the merits of their virtuous activities (good karma) are exhausted, return to the mortal world (Earth). Thus, they, seeking sense pleasures, abiding by the instructions given in the three Vedas, achieve only coming and going (between the heavens and the Earth).

(22) Those who (contrary to the seekers of pleasure), meditating on Me and none other (having no other goal), worship Me, being ever attached to Me, to them I supply what they lack (in their devotion, thus making sure they reach Krishna), and preserve what they possess (their already gathered assets of devotion, thus preventing them from falling down in their spiritual endeavors).

(23) Even the devotees of other gods, who worship them with faith, worship Me only, O Kaunteya, though following the wrong method (of worshipping Krishna *indirectly* through the demigods).

(24) I indeed am the ultimate enjoyer and also the Lord of all sacrifices; but they (the devotees of the demigods) do not know Me in essence; hence they fall down (in their spiritual efforts, resulting in them returning to this mortal world).

(25) The devotees of the demigods go to the demigods; the devotees of the ancestors go to the ancestors; the devotees of the ghosts go to the ghosts; but My devotees come to Me (to stay with Krishna forever).

(26) Whoever offers Me, with devotion, even a leaf, a flower, a fruit, water (the simplest of offerings), I accept that, if it is offered by a pure soul with devotion.

(27) Whatever you do, whatever you eat, whatever you offer (in sacrifice), whatever you give (in charity), whatever austerities you undertake, O Kaunteya — do that as an offering to Me.

(28) Thus, you will be liberated from the bondage of actions yielding auspicious and inauspicious results. With your mind steadfast by the Yoga of renunciation (unattachment to rewards of actions), being freed, you will come to Me.

(29) I am impartial to all beings; to Me no one is detestable, and no one is dear. But those who worship Me with devotion are in Me, and I am also in them (thus they become one with Krishna).

(30) Even if a man of abominable conduct worships Me, devoted to no one else, he should indeed be regarded as a sage, because he is rightly resolved.

(31) He soon becomes righteous and attains eternal peace. O Kaunteya, declare to all that My devotee never perishes.

(32) For, by taking shelter in Me, O Partha, even they, who may be of a so-called sinful birth — women (irrespective of gender), merchants (irrespective of occupation) and labour-class people (irrespective of social status) — can attain the supreme goal (Krishna's association).

(33) How much easier then it is for the righteous Brahmins (knowers of God or the Brahman) and the devoted royal sages. Having come to this temporary, miserable world, worship Me.

(34) Fixing your mind on Me, become My devotee; surrender to Me, and bow down to Me. Absorbing your self thus, and accepting Me as the supreme goal, you will surely come to Me.

It is not difficult to understand why the Blessed Lord refers to the information revealed in this chapter as the "sovereign education," "the sovereign secret," and "the supreme purifier." This is the highest form of knowledge, and the only one that gives the life of a human its meaning. It is known to very few of us, as being born in Kali-Yuga — the dark age — we are least inclined to know our true identities and purpose. This knowledge is so sanctifying that it can purify all of one's sins. And it fulfills the ultimate purpose of religion, which is to help human beings understand and achieve their divine objective.

Krishna also confirms that He is everything, the source of everything, the preserver of everything, and also the annihilator of everything. And we are His children in the sense that we come from Him and possess very small fractions of His qualities.

As Krishna declares, the purpose of the human life is to get rid of the material world permanently and reach the divine world of Krishna — our true home — which is the only way to end our miseries and attain absolute happiness.

Depending on the virtue of our collective actions in all our lives so far, we are assigned our next lives in suitable forms on suitable planets. But that does not imply that the so-called good deeds guarantee liberation. If our actions do not include knowledge of Krishna, faith in Krishna, devotion to Krishna, and meditation on Krishna, then we would only reach heavenly planets (at best) to enjoy the fruits of our good material work, after the exhaustion of which we would need to return to this world to continue our efforts of attaining permanent freedom.

Krishna clarifies that in order to attain Him, we must worship Him directly. If we worship the lesser gods, we worship only Him, but not in the prescribed manner. We might be able to reach heavenly planets this way, but not Krishna's supreme abode.

Simply put, unwavering love for Krishna is what is needed for attaining liberation from this material world, and thereafter living with Him forever — the single true purpose of our lives.

Chapter 10 - The Glories of the Divine One

In the preceding chapter, Lord Krishna touched upon some of the aspects of His divine nature. However, for our benefit, in this chapter, the Lord Himself explains some of the most prominent manifestations of His endless character. This knowledge is blissful for anybody who wants to know God. Although there is no limit to the divine attributes and manifestations of the Lord, and our tiny minds are incapable of comprehending even one-in-a-millionth part of His nature, the Lord still gives a broad enough description of His character so that a true seeker can get a hint of how great He might actually be. Let's dive into this divine wisdom about God.

Lord Krishna (to Arjuna):

(1) O Mahabaho, listen again to My supreme words, which I, wishing your welfare, will speak to you, who delights in hearing Me.

(2) Neither the hosts of demigods nor the great sages know My origin (as, being beyond the limitations of time and space, Krishna has no origin); for, in every way, I am the origin of the demigods and the great sages.

(3) He who knows Me as the unborn and the beginningless, and also as the Supreme Lord of all the worlds — he, among the mortals, is non-deluded, and is liberated from all sins.

(4) Intelligence, knowledge, non-delusion, forgiveness, truthfulness, control of the senses, control of the mind, happiness, sorrow, birth, death, fear, and also fearlessness, ...

(5) ... non-injury (to the innocent), equanimity, contentment, austerity, charity, fame, infamy — all these various attributes of beings arise from Me alone.

(6) The seven great sages (to whom the Vedas were first revealed), the ancient four (mind-born sons of Brahma), and the Manus (the progenitors of mankind), possessing My nature, were born of My mind, and from them all creatures of the world come.

(7) One who truly knows this opulent nature and mystical personality of Mine, becomes unshakably united with Me (by becoming liberated); of this there is no doubt.

(8) I am the source of all (spiritual and material, living and non-living, tangible and intangible);

from Me everything evolves. Thus realizing, the wise engage in worshipping Me with loving devotion.

(9) With minds fixed on Me, with lives devoted to Me, enlightening one another by always conversing about Me, they derive contentment and bliss.

(10) To those who are ever engaged in worshipping Me with love, I grant that intelligence by which they reach Me.

(11) Out of sheer compassion for them, I, dwelling in their hearts, destroy the darkness born of ignorance by the radiant lamp of knowledge.

Arjuna (to Lord Krishna):

(12) You are the Supreme Brahman (the all-powerful God), the supreme abode, the supreme purifier; You are the eternal person, the divine, the original Lord — the unborn, the omnipresent.

(13) All the sages — Narada, the sage of the gods, and also Asita, Devala and Vyasa (the sages of the highest order) confirm this about You; and now You Yourself are declaring this to me.

(14) I accept as truth all that You have told me, O Keshava. Verily, neither the gods nor the demons, O Lord, can understand Your personality.

(15) Indeed, You Yourself know Yourself by Yourself (being the knower of everything), O Purushuttama, O origin of all beings, O Lord of all beings, O God of gods, O Lord of the universe!

(16) You should indeed tell me in detail about Your divine glories — the very glories by which You exist pervading all these worlds.

(17) How shall I know You, O Yogi (Supreme Mystic), constantly thinking of You? In what all forms, O Lord, should You be thought of by me?

(18) O Janardana, please tell me again, in detail, of Your Yoga (mystic power) and opulence; verily, I can never be fully satisfied hearing Your nectar-like words.

Arjuna, regaining some of his composure, realizes that the person standing in front of him, serving him as his charioteer, and guiding him at the moment, is none other than God Himself. Convinced of Krishna's opulence, he accepts the fact completely. Next, he becomes curious to know about the various forms and manifestations of the Lord. Krishna gladly agrees to explain this to him, and through him, to the entire human race.

Lord Krishna (to Arjuna):

(19) Ah yes! O Best of the Kurus, I will certainly tell you My divine glories, but only the prominent ones; for My opulence has no end.

(20) I am the Supreme Soul, O Gudakesha, seated in the hearts of all beings; and I am the beginning, and the middle, and also the end of all beings.

(21) Among the Adityas (twelve luminous beings), I am Vishnu (Krishna's Supreme Form); among the effulgent ones, I am the radiant sun (the most shining one); among the Maruts (wind-gods), I am Marichi (the chief among wind-gods); among the stars, I am the moon (the brightest one in the night).

(22) Among the Vedas, I am the Sama-Veda (the most melodious Veda); among the demigods, I am Vasava (the chief of gods and heaven, Indra); among the senses, I am the mind (the controller of all senses); and I am the consciousness of all the creatures.

(23) Among the Rudras (radiant gods), I am Shankara (their chief); among the Yakshas (nature-spirits) and Rakshasas (ogres), I am Kubera (their king and the lord of wealth); among the Vasus (the eight brilliant beings), I am fire (the most brilliant); and among the mountains, I am Meru (the highest mythological mountain).

(24) Also, among the priests, O Partha, know Me to be their chief, Brihaspati (the divine priest); among the army-generals, I am Skanda (son of Lord Shiva); among water bodies, I am the ocean (the biggest water body which absorbs the water of all smaller water bodies).

(25) Among the great sages, I am Bhrigu (one of the most learned sages); among words, I am the single-syllable-word (*Om* — the cosmic sound vibration); among sacrifices, I am the sacrifice of *japa* (the purifying, meditative, and repetitive chanting of the holy names of God); among immovable things, I am the Himalayas (the firmest of all).

(26) Among all trees, I am the pipal tree (the holy tree that has great religious significance); and among the godly sages, I am Narada (the divine-devotee-form of Vishnu); among the Gandharvas (the divine singers), I am Citraratha (the best singer among Gandharvas); among perfected beings, I am sage Kapila (the author of the Sankhya philosophy — the knowledge-based path to Krishna).

(27) Among horses, know Me to be Uchhaishravas (the divine horse), born of nectar (during the churning of the ocean for the immortality-giving nectar); among godly elephants, know Me to be Airavata (the divine white elephant born from the same churning); and among men, know Me to be the king (the Lord of all beings).

(28) Among weapons, I am the thunderbolt (the most luminous and powerful destroyer); among cows, I am Kamadhuk (the desire-fulfilling cow born of the ocean-churning); I am Kandarpa (Cupid, the god of love), the cause for offspring; and among serpents, I am Vasuki (the serpent of Lord Shiva).

(29) Among the Nagas (many-hooded serpents), I am Ananta (also called Sheshanaag, the thousand-hooded divine serpent which forms the bed of Vishnu, Krishna's Supreme Form); among the aquatic beings, I am Varuna (the god of water); among the ancestors, I am Aryama (the god of the world of ancestors); and among the regulators, I am Yama (the god of death).

(30) And, among demons, I am Prahlada (who, though born in a demon family, was a great devotee of Krishna); among reckoners, I am time (which ultimately neutralizes everything); and among animals, I am the lion (the king of animals); and among birds, I am Garuda (the divine king of birds and the vehicle of Vishnu).

(31) Among purifiers, I am air (capable of carrying away all the dust of ignorance); among the wielders of weapons, I am Rama (the greatest warrior and the best among men, a previous incarnation of Krishna); and among fishes, I am the shark (the most dangerous of fishes); among rivers, I am the Ganges (the divine river, a symbol of purity).

(32) Among creations, I am the beginning and the end, and also the middle, O Arjuna; among knowledge, I am the knowledge of the self; among debaters, I am the logic (the natural basis of conclusion).

(33) Among letters, I am the letter 'A' (the beginning of language); and among compound words, I am the dual compound (pair of two words, often used to signify the relationships with Krishna, like Radha-Krishna); I am also infinite time (signifying Krishna's eternal nature); I am the creator facing all sides (Brahma — Krishna's creator form).

(34) I am also the all-devouring death, and I am the origin of all that is yet to be; among feminine attributes (of nature), I am fame, beauty, speech, memory, intelligence, steadfastness, and forgiveness.

(35) And among hymns, I am Brihat-Sama (the difficult-to-sing divine hymns of the Sama-Veda);

among poetic meters, I am Gayatri (the most chanted Vedic mantra); among months, I am Marga-Shirsha (the refreshing winter month); among seasons, I am the flowery spring (the most relaxing season).

(36) Of the frauds, I am gambling (the one who deceives the deceivers by destroying them); I am the splendor of the splendid; I am victory, I am effort; I am the purity of the pure.

(37) Among the Vrishnis (descendants of Vrishni), I am Vasudeva; and among the Pandavas, I am Dhananjaya (Arjuna); among the sages, I am Vyasa (the compiler of the entire Vedic literature); among poets (great thinkers and seers), I am the savant Ushana (also known as Shukra, the learned preceptor of the demons).

(38) Among means to discipline, I am punishment (the final way to discipline one); of the seekers of victory, I am the righteous principles (following which only can make one truly victorious); and also of secret things, I am silence (the most confidential one); I am the knowledge of the men of knowledge.

(39) Also, whatsoever is the seed (origin) of all beings, that am I, O Arjuna. There is nothing — moving or nonmoving — that can exist without Me.

(40) There is no limit to My divine glories, O Parantapa. All this has been spoken by Me as a mere indication of the expanse of those glories.

(41) Whatever exists that is glorious, prosperous, or energetic, you should know all those to have certainly born of just a fragment of My splendor.

(42) However, O Arjuna, what is the need for you to know all this in such detail? For it is sufficient to simply understand that I remain supporting this entire universe with merely a single fragment of Myself.

The Lord thus explains His divine manifestations in the most perfect and detailed manner possible. There could not be a better way to do this other than Him being as direct and straightforward as He has been. He is everywhere and in everything. Everything comes from Him, everything remains in Him, and everything is destroyed by Him. He is everything and everything is Him. Nothing more needs to be said in this regard.

Chapter 11 - The Universal Form of God

This is the chapter for all those who want to know the *real* form of God — how He actually looks. Having realized that Krishna is the Supreme God, Arjuna requests Him to show him His actual cosmic form — the form nobody has ever seen before — the form even the demigods do not have the good fortune of beholding. And, for the benefit of the entire human race, the kind Lord agrees to fulfill that wish of Arjuna. This chapter contains a vivid description of that divine, all-encompassing, gigantic, but terrifying form of the Supreme God.

Arjuna (to Lord Krishna):

(1) By hearing that speech — the highest secret pertaining to the Supreme Self — uttered by You for my benefit, this delusion of mine has been dispelled.

(2) O Lotus-eyed One, I have verily heard from You in detail about the appearance and disappearance of all beings, and also Your limitless glories.

(3) O Supreme Lord! As You have thus spoken about Yourself, I wish to behold Your divine form, O Purushuttama.

(4) If You think, O Lord, that it is possible to be seen by me, O Lord of Yoga, then kindly show me Your eternal Self.

Lord Krishna (to Arjuna):

(5) Behold, O Partha, hundreds and thousands of My varied forms — divine, and of various colors and shapes.

(6) O descendant of Bharata, behold the Adityas, the Vasus, the Rudras, the Ashwins, and the Maruts (and all the other demigods). Behold also the many wonders never seen by anyone before.

(7) O Gudakesha, behold in My body the entire universe together at the same place, including the moving and the non-moving, and whatever else you wish to see.

(8) But you cannot see Me with merely these eyes of yours; therefore, I give to you divine eyes; with those eyes behold My mystical opulence!

Our senses are too limited. We cannot see God with our material eyes. We can only feel His presence, just like we can feel the air around us. But it's a pity that we have no issues believing in the presence of air, but do not really care about knowing the truths about God. Krishna thus provides Arjuna with divine eyes so that he could see His cosmic form as it is, and describe it for the benefit of the coming generations.

Sanjaya (to Dhritarashtra):

(9) O King, having spoken thus, the Supreme Lord of Yoga, Hari (Krishna), displayed His supreme opulent form to Partha (Arjuna).

(10) Having many mouths and eyes, possessing many wonderful sights, adorned with many divine ornaments, holding many divine uplifted weapons, ...

(11) ... wearing divine garlands and dresses, anointed with divine fragrances — all-wonderful, brilliant, unlimited, looking in all directions.

(12) If a thousand suns were present in the sky at the same time, that combined radiance might resemble the effulgence of Him — the Supreme Self.

(13) There, in the body of the God of gods, Pandava (Arjuna) then saw the entire universe, divided in many, all at one place.

(14) Then, he, Dhananjaya (Arjuna), overwhelmed with wonder, with hairs standing on end, bowed his head to the Lord, and with joined palms, spoke.

Arjuna (to Lord Krishna):

(15) O Lord, I see all the gods in Your body, and all classes of beings too; I also see Lord Brahma (the god of creation), sitting on the lotus (his seat), and also all the sages and divine serpents.

(16) O Lord of the world, O universal form, I see You, of endless form, on all sides, with many arms, bellies, mouths, and eyes, having no end, no middle, and also no beginning.

(17) I see You with crown, club, and disc; a mass of effulgence glowing all around, very difficult to behold, blazing radiance everywhere like fire or the sun, and incomprehensible.

(18) You are imperishable and the supreme one to be known; You are the ultimate repository of this universe; You are inexhaustible; You are the protector of Sanatana Dharma (the eternal religion); You are the eternal person. This is my opinion.

(19) I see You having no origin, middle, and end, infinite in power, having innumerable arms, having the moon and the sun as eyes, with blazing fire coming out from Your mouth, heating this whole universe by Your own radiance.

(20) Indeed, this space between the heavens and the earth is pervaded by You alone, and so are all the directions. O Supreme Soul, after seeing Your wonderful, terrible form, all the three worlds are perturbed.

(21) Verily, all those hosts of gods are entering into You; some of them, out of fear, extol You with joined palms. Hosts of great sages and perfected beings are praising You with sublime hymns, saying, "May it be well!"

(22) The Rudras, the Adityas, the Vasus, and the Sadhyas, the Vishvadevas, the two Ashwins, the Maruts, and the Usmapas, and the Gandharvas, the Yakshas, the Asuras, the Siddhas — they all (these groups of the different classes of gods and demons) are beholding You, indeed in wonder.

(23) O Mighty-armed, seeing Your immense form with many mouths and eyes, many arms, thighs, and feet, many bellies, looking horrible with many teeth, all the worlds are terrified, and so am I.

(24) O Vishnu, indeed, seeing You touching the sky, blazing with many colors, open-mouthed, with large fiery eyes, I, being terrified within, cannot find steadiness and peace.

(25) Seeing these mouths of Yours with terrible teeth, resembling the fire of death, I have lost my sense of direction, nor can I find comfort. Be gracious, O Devesha, O shelter of the universe!

(26) Also, all these sons of Dhritarashtra, along with hosts of kings of earth, and also Bhishma, Drona, and the son of charioteer (Karna), with our prominent warriors too, ...

(27) ... are rapidly entering into Your mouths with terribly fearsome teeth. Some of them are seen sticking in the gaps between the teeth, with their heads crushed.

(28) Verily, as the many torrents of the waters of the rivers flow toward the ocean, so also these heroes of the human world are entering into Your blazing mouths.

(29) As moths rush hastily into a blazing fire for their own destruction, so also are all creatures of the world dashing into Your mouths for their own destruction.

(30) You are licking Your lips, devouring all creatures from all sides with blazing mouths, covering the whole world with effulgence. Your fierce rays are scorching, O Vishnu.

(31) Tell me who You are, so fierce in form. Obeisances unto You, O Supreme God; please be gracious. I desire to know You, the original one; I, indeed, do not know Your purpose.

As the Lord had indicated, Arjuna sees all and everything inside that universal form of Krishna.

He sees beings being created as well as getting annihilated. He sees all the demigods, all the demons, all the creatures, all the celestial planets and stars — the entire creation — all at one place, inside that massive body. This makes it very evident to Arjuna that Krishna is everything — the origin, the middle, and the end.

Lord Krishna (to Arjuna):

(32) I am time, the mighty destroyer of the worlds, now engaged in annihilating the creatures here (in this battlefield). Even without you, all the warriors arrayed in the confronting armies will cease to exist.

(33) Therefore, get up and gain glory. Conquering the enemies, enjoy a prosperous kingdom. Verily, all of them have already been killed by Me; be you merely an instrument, O Savyasachi.

(34) Drona, and Bhishma, and Jayadratha, and Karna, and the other brave warriors have been already killed by Me; so you shall slay them without grief. Fight! You shall conquer your enemies in battle.

Whatsoever Krishna intends is what actually happens, regardless of what we wish to see happening. Our job is to perform our duties to the best of our abilities. This is our responsibility.

Whatever Krishna desires would be the ultimate result. That is not something for us to worry about.

Sanjaya (to Dhritarashtra):

(35) After hearing this speech of Keshava (Krishna), the trembling Kiriti (Arjuna), with joined palms, prostrating himself, bowing down, overwhelmed with fear, said again to Krishna with a faltering voice.

Arjuna (to Lord Krishna):

(36) It is proper, O Hrishikesha, that the world rejoices in and becomes attracted by Your glories; that the demons, out of Your fear, run in all directions; and also that all groups of the perfected sages bow down to You.

(37) And why should not they pay homage, O Great Soul, to You, to the first creator, who is even greater than Brahma (as Brahma also comes from Krishna)? O limitless one, O God of gods, O shelter of the universe! You are the imperishable one, the manifest, the unmanifest, the transcendental.

(38) You are the primal God, the oldest person; You are the supreme refuge of this universe. You are the knower, the knowable (the only one worthy of being known), and the supreme abode.

O being of unlimited forms, the universe is pervaded by You!

(39) You are air, death, fire, water, and the moon! You are Prajapati (the Lord of all beings) and the great-grandfather (the oldest one). Salutation! Salutation be unto You a thousand times, again and again! Salutation! Salutation to You!

(40) Salutation to You from the front and from behind; Salutation to You from all sides indeed, O Everything; You are infinite in power, infinite in prowess; You pervade everything; therefore, You are everything.

(41) Whatever I said rashly to You, not knowing this greatness of Yours, regarding You as merely a friend, either out of carelessness, or out of love, addressing You as, "O Krishna," "O Yadava," "O friend," etc.; ...

(42) ... and, O Achyuta, howsoever You have been insulted by me for fun — while playing, while laying down on bed, while sitting, or while eating, in private, or even in company — for all that I beg pardon of You, O immeasurable one.

(43) You are the father of the world — of the moving and the nonmoving; You are also its glorious preceptor, worthy of worship. There is no one equal to You; then how can there be anyone superior to You in the three worlds, O Lord of unequalled power?

(44) Therefore, laying down, prostrating the body, I beg Your forgiveness, O adorable Lord. As does a father to his son, as a friend to his friend, as a lover to his beloved, so should You forgive me, O God.

We often do not treat God the way He should be treated. Some regard themselves as all-powerful, believing that their 'success' is solely due to their own efforts. Some regard God as a supplier of their objects of desire. Some even call Him names when He does not provide them with what they desire. And some simply do not believe in His existence. But, sooner or later, we must all come to terms with the truths about God's nature and authority. Keeping this in mind, we should never do something that may require us to feel guilty about our grave error at the time of realization.

(45) I am delighted by seeing what has never before been seen; but also, my mind is unsettled with fear (seeing such a horrible form). O Lord, please show that previous form to me; be gracious, O Lord of lords, O shelter of the universe.

(46) I wish to behold You as before — crowned, wielding a mace, with disc in hand, in at least that four-handed form (if not the human-like two handed form); please appear thus, O thousand-armed one, O Vishvamurte.

Krishna's cosmic form, though transcendental, mystical, and grand, is difficult to love for our minds. Our human minds are not made in a way that they can fall in love with someone who is as horrible-looking as God's universal form. This form has many mouths with gigantic jaws, between which the dead are seen hanging with their heads smashed, stained in blood. This is obviously not a form of deity we can easily worship with love. Therefore, fearful of this massive form of the Lord, Arjuna begs Him to return to His previous human-like form, which is ideal for love and worship. He is even open to behold the Lord in His four-handed form, which is almost as gentle as His two-handed form, and certainly far less terrifying than His current cosmic form.

Lord Krishna (to Arjuna):

(47) Happily by Me, O Arjuna, through My own internal powers, has been shown to you this supreme form of Mine — effulgent, cosmic, infinite, primeval — that has not been seen before by anyone.

(48) Neither by the study of the Vedas and by making sacrifices, nor by giving gifts, nor by following rituals, nor by practicing severe austerities, can I be perceived in this form in this mortal world by anyone other than you, O bravest of the Kurus.

(49) May you have no fear, and may you not be bewildered by seeing such a horrible form of Mine as this. Becoming free from fear, pleased in mind again, behold this earlier form of Mine.

Sanjaya (to Dhritarashtra):

(50) Thus, Vasudeva (Krishna), having thus spoken to Arjuna in that manner, again displayed His own form, and the Great Soul, becoming serene in form again, reassured the terrified one (Arjuna).

Arjuna (to Lord Krishna):

(51) O Janardana, seeing this serene human-like form of Yours, I am now composed in mind, and restored to my own nature.

Lord Krishna (to Arjuna):

(52) This form of Mine which you have seen is very difficult to behold. Even the gods are ever longing to see this form.

(53) Neither by studying the Vedas, nor by undergoing penances, nor by doing charity, nor even by making sacrifices, can I be seen in this form in which you have seen Me.

(54) But, by single-minded devotion, can I, in this form, be known and seen in essence, O Arjuna, and also be entered into, O Parantapa.

(55) O Pandava, one who works for Me (dedicates his actions to Krishna), makes Me the supreme goal, is devoted to Me, is free from material attachment, and is free from enmity toward all beings, certainly comes to Me.

Being steadfast in Yoga is the only way to reach Lord Krishna. We ought to work for Him, giving up the desire for rewards of our actions. We ought to meditate on His loving Krishna-form in full knowledge of Him. And we ought to be ever engaged in His devotion. This way we shall surely attain Krishna.

Chapter 12 - The Yoga of Devotion

Which form of Krishna should one worship has long been a point of contention. Should we worship Krishna in His human-like personal form, or should we worship Him thinking of Him as a 'power' without any form — the impersonal, the unmanifested? The truth is that there is no need for such a debate because the Lord has already delivered His advice in the Bhagavad Gita. Let us see what He says.

Arjuna (to Lord Krishna):

(1) Those devotees who, thus being ever engaged, worship You (Krishna's personal form), and also those who worship the imperishable and unmanifest (Krishna's impersonal form) — which of them are better versed in Yoga?

Lord Krishna (to Arjuna):

(2) Those who, fixing their minds on Me, worship Me (Krishna's personal form), ever steadfast, endowed with great faith, are considered by Me to be the most perfect in Yoga.

(3) But those who fully worship the imperishable, the indefinable, the unmanifest, the all-pervading, the inconceivable, and the changeless, the immovable, the constant, ...

(4) ... by disciplining all the senses, being even-minded everywhere, engaged in the welfare of all beings, they also verily attain Me.

(5) Trouble is much greater for those whose minds are attached to the unmanifested (Krishna's impersonal form); for, the goal, the unmanifest, is difficult to be attained for the embodied soul.

(6) But those who worship Me (Krishna's personal form), dedicating all their activities to Me, accepting Me as the supreme, meditating on Me with single-minded devotion, ...

(7) ... O Partha, for them whose minds are fixed upon Me, I become, before long, the deliverer out of the ocean of mortal deaths.

So, the verdict is clear. Lord Krishna clearly asserts that it is extremely difficult for us humans to perceive anything that has no shape and form. Then how is it possible for our minds, too limited in capacity, to love someone we cannot even see or imagine? Therefore, the Lord advises that we, as seekers, think of Him in His Krishna-like form, which is exceedingly easy to love and worship.

Liberation is a rare gift and is meant to be attained only by the most deserving. But who among so many mortal beings fit the definition of 'most deserving' and thus can expect to attain Krishna, leaving the material world forever? The answer is, "those who are dear to Krishna." And in the following verses, the Lord Himself defines who are the ones who are most dear to Him.

(8) Fix your mind on Me alone, place your intelligence in Me; thereafter, there is no doubt that you will always dwell in Me alone (by attaining liberation).

(9) If, however, you are not able to fix your mind upon Me steadily, O Dhananjaya, seek to attain Me by the Yoga of practice (of bringing the focus back to Krishna).

(10) If you are unable even to practice, be intent on working for Me (by dedicating all actions to Krishna); for by even working for My sake, you will attain perfection.

(11) If you are unable to do even this, then taking shelter in Me, renounce the results of all work, being self-controlled.

(12) Knowledge (Jnana Yoga) is indeed superior to practice (of mind-control); meditation (Raja Yoga or Dhyana Yoga) is superior to knowledge; renunciation of rewards of actions (Karma Yoga) is superior to meditation; peace immediately follows renunciation.

(13) One who is not hateful toward any being, is friendly and compassionate, has no belief in proprietorship (does not consider himself to be the owner of any material object) and is free from ego, is the same in sorrow and happiness, is forgiving, ...

(14) ... is ever content, is a Yogi (always connected to God), is self-controlled, has firm determination (to excel in Yoga), has dedicated his mind and intelligence to Me — he, who is thus a devotee of Mine, is dear to Me.

(15) One by whom the world is not agitated, and who is not agitated by the world, who is free from the emotions of joy, sorrow, fear, and anxiety, is dear to Me.

(16) One who has no expectations (material desires), is pure, is proficient (in the practice of Yoga), is unconcerned (about the results of his actions), is free from sorrow (being established in knowledge), has renounced all commencements (of work with material motives) — he, who is thus a devotee of Mine, is dear to Me.

(17) One who does not rejoice, does not hate, does not lament, does not crave (does not hanker for sense-objects), renounces the dualities of good and evil (accepting everything as Krishna's wish), being filled with devotion, is dear to Me.

(18) One who is the same to foe and friend, so also in honor and dishonor, is the same in cold, heat, happiness, and sorrow, is free from all material attachment, ...

(19) ... is the same in denunciation and praise, remains silent (composed and non-complaining), content with anything (that comes his way), homeless (not caring for a residence other than Krishna's heart), is steady-minded, full of devotion – such a person is dear to Me.

(20) But those who pursue this immortal religion, as declared (in this divine song), and being endowed with faith, consider Me as the supreme one — such devotees are exceedingly dear to Me.

In conclusion, a seeker should begin by gaining knowledge about the soul, the Supreme Soul (God), the relationship between the two, and his purpose in this material life. Armed with such knowledge, he should then try to focus his mind on Krishna. Once he establishes himself in thoughts about Krishna, he should dedicate all his actions and their results to Krishna. This will purify his mind and heart, making him fit for the ultimate stage of Yoga — Bhakti Yoga — to remain constantly engaged in Krishna's devotion.

Along the way, he must keep his senses and emotional turbulences in check, and must keep his mind steady and focused in all situations. Once a Yogi is thus established perfectly in the state of devotional practice, the next stage for him is liberation from the mortal world and attainment of Krishna's association.

Krishna has provided us with the roadmap. Now it is up to us to abide by His clear instructions.

Chapter 13 - The Nature and the Soul

Arjuna's mind becomes somewhat stable as he listens to Lord Krishna's magnificent discourse. He becomes absorbed in Krishna's teachings and seeks to learn more.

Arjuna (to Lord Krishna):

(1) The '*Prakriti*' (material nature) and the 'Supreme Spirit,' the 'field,' and the 'knower of the field,' 'knowledge' and the 'object of knowledge' — all of these I wish to learn, O Keshava.

Lord Krishna (to Arjuna):

(2) This body, O Kaunteya, is called the 'field,' and one who knows the truth of it is called 'knower of the field' by those (learned sages) who know them.

(3) Know Me as the knower of the field in all the fields, O descendant of Bharata. Knowledge of the field and also of the knower of the field is 'knowledge' in My opinion.

(4) What that field is, how it is, what are its changes (forms), whence it is produced, who He (the knower of the field) is, and what His powers are — all that hear from Me in brief.

(5) The seers have sung (about the field and the knower of the field) in many ways, in various hymns (Vedic verses), and also by the rational and convincing words (in the Vedas) indicative of the Brahman (the Supreme God).

(6) The five great elements, ego (identification with the body), intelligence, and also the unmanifested (modes of material nature), the ten senses and the one (the mind), and the five objects of the senses, ...

(7) ... desire, hatred, happiness, sorrow, the aggregate of all these, consciousness, fortitude — the field, with its modifications (various forms), have thus been described in brief.

(8) Humility, unpretentiousness, non-injury (to the innocent), tolerance, sincerity, service of the guru, cleanliness, steadfastness, self-control, ...

(9) ... indifference in regard to the objects of the senses, and also absence of ego, perception of the evils of birth, death, old age, disease, (and the resulting) sorrow, ...

(10) ... non-attachment and non-association (mental detachment) with son, wife, home, etc., and constant even-mindedness on the attainment of the desirable as well as the undesirable, ...

(11) ... and unalloyed devotion unto Me, without separation, inclination to live in a solitary place, distaste for society of people, ...

(12) ... steadfastness in the knowledge of the self (as a soul), contemplation on the goal of true knowledge — all this is declared to be 'knowledge,' and all that is other than this is 'ignorance.'

(13) I will now speak of that which should be known, and knowing which one attains immortality — that beginningless Supreme Brahman called neither being nor non-being.

(14) That has hands and feet everywhere, has eyes, heads and mouths everywhere, has ears everywhere, and exists in the world enveloping everything.

(15) Shining through the functions of all the senses, yet devoid of senses; unattached, yet, verily, the maintainer of all; without material attributes, yet the experiencer of those attributes.

(16) Existing outside and inside all beings, the unmoving and the moving, That is unknowable due to being very subtle; That is near, and also is far (because That is everywhere).

(17) And though actually undivided, That Supreme Soul appears as if divided in all beings (as individual souls). That maintainer of all beings should also be understood to be the devourer and the originator (of everything and everyone).

(18) That is the light even of the lights; That is said to be beyond darkness (ignorance); That is the knowledge, the object of knowledge, to be reached by knowledge; That is seated in the hearts of all (as individual souls).

(19) Thus, the 'field,' and the 'knowledge,' as well as the 'object of knowledge' have been briefly described. Understanding this, My devotee enters My nature.

In essence, Krishna declares that only someone who understands Him as the Supreme Soul and his own true identity as an individual soul is worthy of being called to enlightenment. To be truly successful in life, we must first understand ourselves. Following that, we should work on cultivating virtues like mental detachment, humility, sincerity, and, most importantly, steadfastness in our devotion to Krishna. We must see Krishna as the all-pervading maintainer and enjoyer, as well as the one and only true object of knowledge. Everything else must be regarded as ignorance.

Krishna continues to impart His diving teachings to Arjuna:

(20) Know both the material nature and the soul to be, verily, without a beginning. Know the modifications as well as the attributes to be born of material nature.

(21) With regard to the creation of effect and cause, material nature is said to be the cause (of all material effects); in the matter of experiencing happiness and sorrow, the individual nature of the particular material being is said to be the cause.

(22) The individual soul, situated in material nature, verily experiences the attributes born of material nature. Contact with the specific attributes (in its current life) is the cause (deciding factor) of its next birth in good or evil wombs.

(23) The transcendental person in this body is also spoken of as the spectator, the permitter, and the maintainer, the enjoyer, the Great Lord, and also the Supreme Soul.

(24) One who thus knows the being and the material nature, along with the attributes (of material nature), in whatsoever situation, will not take birth again (in this material world).

(25) Some, by Dhyana (Yoga of meditation), see the Supreme Self in the individual self (soul) by the self (mind); others by Sankhya Yoga (Yoga of knowledge); and others by Karma Yoga (Yoga of action).

(26) Others, however, not knowing this, worship Me, hearing about Me from others (wise sages). They too, devoted to hearing about Me, verily, cross beyond death (by attaining liberation through this Yoga of worship — Bhakti Yoga).

(27) O best among the descendants of Bharata, whatever object comes into being, unmoving or moving, know that to be coming from the union of the 'field' and the 'knower of the field.'

(28) He actually sees who sees the Supreme Lord existing equally in all beings — the imperishable existing in the perishable.

(29) Indeed, he who sees the Lord equally situated everywhere does not destroy the self (awareness of being a soul) by the self (false ego of being independently situated), and therefore attains the supreme goal (of Lord's companionship).

(30) And he sees who sees that all action is indeed performed in all respects by material nature alone, and the Self (God) is the non-doer.

(31) When one realizes that the diversity of beings is actually situated in the One, and spreads forth therefrom, he then attains the state (nature) of the Brahman.

(32) Being without beginning, and being devoid of material attributes, this imperishable Supreme Self, though dwelling in the body, O Kaunteya, neither acts, nor is tainted (by the effects of Karma).

(33) As the all-pervading space, because of its subtlety, is not tainted, so too the self (the individual soul), though situated everywhere in the body, is not tainted.

(34) As the one sun illuminates this whole world, similarly the 'knower of the field' illuminates (gives life to) the whole 'field,' O descendant of Bharata.

(35) They who, through the eye of knowledge, know thus the difference between the 'field' and the 'knower of the field,' and understand the process of attaining liberation from the 'nature of the being' (material nature), reach the Supreme (by thus achieving liberation).

In this way, Lord Krishna beautifully exposes the truth about and the relationship between Himself and us, the created material beings. Being outside the dimensions of time and space, He is eternal and unborn. He is the Brahman — the everlasting, all-pervading, all-powerful Supreme Soul. And He has created all beings, whether dwelling on Earth or elsewhere (like gods and demons). Each of such created beings carries a minuscule part of that infinite Supreme Soul as a tiny individual soul.

The Lord is also the creator of *Prakriti* — His material nature. When a soul comes into contact with material nature, it loses its memory, forgets who it is, and attaches itself to material objects and to other similarly deluded souls.

We must understand, as Krishna declares, that He, in His superior nature, does not engage in any material activity. Only His material nature (Prakriti) is active in the material world. The contact with material nature evokes a range of feelings and emotions, such as happiness and sorrow. We must rise above those, as suggested by Krishna multiple times in the Bhagavad Gita. Rising above these emotions, born of material nature, is crucial for attaining liberation. In fact, it is the attachment resulting from contact with nature that causes continuous rebirths in various kinds of wombs, until the soul attains the necessary wisdom and works to liberate itself.

Therefore, our task is to realize who we are and get back to where we have come from — God's supreme abode. There are several ways to do it — gaining knowledge about God and the soul, meditating on the Lord, working for the Lord, and engaging oneself in Lord's devotion wholeheartedly.

In the following chapter, the kind Lord expands on the various kinds of attributes of material nature, the best among them, and our role in relation to these diverse attributes.

Chapter 14 - The Three Modes of Material Nature

In the previous chapter, Lord Krishna touched upon the meaning and significance of Prakriti in the material world. Prakriti is nothing but Supreme Lord Krishna's material nature, which keeps this whole world running. In this chapter, He elaborates on this subject, introducing us to the various modes in which His material nature functions, how these modes are different from one another, and how we should use this knowledge for our own spiritual advancement.

Lord Krishna (to Arjuna):

(1) I shall speak again of the supreme knowledge, the best of all knowledge, having known which all the sages have attained the highest perfection from here (after leaving this world).

(2) They who, taking refuge in this knowledge, have attained the same nature as Mine, are not born even during creation, nor suffer pain during annihilation (thus they become ever free from and indifferent to the cycle of births and deaths).

(3) My womb is the great Brahma (the god of material creation); in that I place the seed; from that all beings take birth, O descendant of Bharata.

(4) Whichever forms of material life originate in all the wombs, O Kaunteya, the great Brahma is their true womb (making him the mother in a sense), and I am the seed-giving father.

(5) *Sattva* (the mode of purity), *Rajas* (the mode of passion), *Tamas* (the mode of darkness) — these *Gunas* (attributes) born of *Prakriti* (material nature) bind the imperishable, embodied one (the soul) in the body, O Mahabaho.

(6) Of these (three modes of material nature), the mode of purity, being immaculate, is illuminating and harmless (as it does not cause sin). It, however, binds (the soul to the material world) through attachment to material happiness and attachment to knowledge, O Anagha.

(7) Know the mode of passion to be of the nature of ecstasy born of lust and attachment. O Kaunteya, it binds (the soul to the material world) through attachment to action (carried out with the objective of sense satisfaction).

(8) But know the mode of darkness to be born of ignorance, which deludes all embodied beings. O descendant of Bharata, it binds (the soul to the material world) through heedlessness, laziness, and sleep.

(9) The mode of purity attaches to material happiness, the mode of passion to action, O Bharata, while the mode of darkness, shrouding knowledge, attaches, indeed, to heedlessness.

(10) O descendant of Bharata, purity rises by overpowering passion and darkness (in one's mind); passion by overpowering purity and darkness; and similarly, darkness by overpowering purity and passion.

(11) When the illumination of knowledge radiates through all the gates (senses) in this body, then it may be known that the mode of purity has increased predominantly.

(12) Greed, activity, undertaking of actions, restlessness, hankering — these arise when the mode of passion becomes predominant, O best among the descendants of Bharata.

(13) Absence of light (of wisdom), inactivity, heedlessness, and also delusion — these arise when the mode of darkness becomes predominant, O beloved child of the Kurus.

(14) When an embodied one undergoes death while the mode of purity is predominant (in his mind), then he attains to the spotless worlds of the 'knowers of the highest' (like the learned sages).

(15) Undergoing death in the predominant mode of passion, one is born among those attached to action. Similarly, dying in the predominant mode of darkness, one is born in the womb of the unintelligent (like animals, etc.).

(16) The result of action in the mode of purity is said to be pure and immaculate; but the result of action in the mode of passion is sorrow; and the result of action in the mode of darkness is even more ignorance.

(17) From the mode of purity arises knowledge; greed, surely, from the mode of passion; heedlessness, delusion, and also ignorance, verily, from the mode of darkness.

(18) Those who are situated in the mode of purity go upwards (to the heavenly planets); those who are situated in the mode of passion dwell in the middle (in the earthly planets); those who are situated in the abominable mode of darkness go downwards (to the hellish planets).

(19) When a seer sees no other performer than the modes of material nature, and knows Him (Supreme God) who is higher than these modes, he attains My nature.

(20) The embodied (the soul) having transcended these three modes of material nature, from which the body originates, is freed from birth, death, decay (old age), and sorrows (resulting from them), and experiences immortality.

Sattva (purity), *Rajas* (passion), and *Tamas* (darkness) — without comprehending these three modes of material nature, a seeker's understanding of how the material world works and what keeps it going remains incomplete.

When one's mind is fixed in the knowledge of oneself and God, and he thereby loses interest in material gains and possessions, he establishes himself in the mode of purity. On the contrary, when one becomes overly devoted to the experiences of his senses, considering their satisfaction to be the goal of his existence, and acts accordingly, he is said to be established in the mode of passion. And worse, if one resorts to unethical behavior, disregards morality and self-control, and lives solely for the gratification of his lusty senses, he is said to be living in the mode of darkness.

The mode in which one is established at the time of death is critical in deciding his next destination and the womb in which he shall take his next birth. Hence, it is absolutely essential for a seeker to understand these three modes and their unique attributes, and try to live steadfast in the mode of purity. However, though establishing oneself in the mode of purity elevates one to godly planets, it also assures that one would return to the material world after enjoying his time in the world of gods, and resume his quest for liberation, which is his true goal.

To ensure that we get liberated from this material world after our current lives, reaching Krishna's abode without delay, and dwelling there forever, we must transcend *all* three modes, including the mode of purity. But how do we do that? Arjuna has the same question for the Lord.

Arjuna (to Lord Krishna):

(21) By what signs is one who has transcended these three modes of material nature known, O Lord? What is his behavior, and how does he transcend these three modes of material nature?

Lord Krishna (to Arjuna):

(22) O Pandava, he neither hates illumination (knowledge), activity, and delusion (the respective characteristics of the three modes of material nature) when these are present, nor longs for these when these are absent.

(23) One who, seated like one indifferent, is not disturbed by the modes of material nature; who, knowing that the modes act alone, remains firm and does not swerve; ...

(24) ... alike in sorrow and happiness; situated in the self (the knowledge of being a soul); to whom a lump of earth, stone, and gold are the same; to whom the pleasant and the unpleasant are the same; equally firm in criticism and praise of oneself; ...

(25) ... who is same in honor and dishonor; who is equally on the side of a friend and a foe; who has abandoned all undertakings (with a desire for rewards) — he is said to have transcended the modes of material nature.

(26) And one who serves Me, without swerving, through Bhakti Yoga (Yoga of devotion), he, having transcended the modes of material nature, qualifies to become one with the Brahman (through liberation), ...

(27) ... for I am the abode of the Brahman — the immortal, and the imperishable, the eternal, the virtuous, and the absolute bliss.

The Lord makes it very clear that only one who remains oblivious to the never-ending waves of the material ocean can cross it by being established in Yoga of devotion to Krishna. An intelligent person who understands the meaninglessness of the ebb and flow that defines this material world and consequently remains unconcerned about it, always engrossed in worshiping the Lord, will undoubtedly reach His abode.

Chapter 15 - The Supreme Person

We now understand that our purpose in life is to attain freedom from this material world to live forever in the blissful company of Lord Krishna. But do we still have a clear understanding of who Lord Krishna is? Krishna has revealed a lot about Himself in the preceding chapters, as well as His actual cosmic form, which proves that He is all-encompassing. But we humans will never be able to comprehend Him fully. That is why the Lord goes into further detail about His traits in this chapter, as well as our relationship with Him and how we should perceive Him.

Lord Krishna (to Arjuna):

(1) They (the wise people) say that the *pipal* tree (the material world), which has its roots (unmanifested divine consciousness) upward and branches (nature, modes of nature, attributes of these modes, senses, mind, etc., along with their manifestations like desire, ego, pleasure, etc.) downward, and of which the Vedas are the leaves (protector), is imperishable (being a reflection of the spiritual world); he who knows that is the knower of the Vedas.

(2) The branches (the various elements of nature) of that (*pipal* tree — the material world) are spread downward (in the lower beings like humans, animals, plants, etc.) and upward (in the demigods up to Brahma), nourished by the modes of material nature, having sense-objects as their twigs (the effects of the three modes). And downward, in the human world, stretch forth the roots (beings as a part of the divine), bound by material actions (Karma causing beings to return to this world again and again).

(3) Its (the tree's) form is not perceived here (in this world) as such — neither the end, nor the beginning, nor even the foundation. After cutting down the strong-rooted *pipal* tree with the mighty weapon of detachment, ...

(4) ... that condition (liberation) has to be sought for, reaching which, no one returns again. Take refuge in Him — the Primeval Person (God) alone, from whom has ensued everything from time immemorial.

(5) Free from pride and delusion, having conquered the evil of attachment, absorbed constantly in the self, unattached to desires, free from dualities such as happiness and sorrow — the undeluded attain that imperishable state (of liberation).

(6) Neither the sun illuminates that, nor the moon, nor fire, reaching which they (the liberated souls) do not return; that is My supreme abode (called Vaikuntha).

(7) It is verily a fragment of Mine which, becoming the eternal soul in the living being, in the world of living beings, situated in the material nature, draws to itself the six senses, including the mind.

(8) When the Lord obtains a body (as an individual soul), and thereafter leaves it, He takes these (six senses, including the mind) and goes away, as air carries away the fragrances from their sources (flowers).

(9) Presiding over the ear, the eye, the touch (skin), the taste (tongue), and the smell (nose), as also the mind, He enjoys the sense-objects (being the ultimate enjoyer).

(10) The deluded cannot see Him departing (as the soul from the body), dwelling (in the body), enjoying (through the senses and the mind), or associating with the modes of material nature. Those with the eyes of knowledge can see.

(11) The striving Yogis also see Him (the Lord) situated in the self (the soul). But the impure and the unintelligent, even though striving, do not see Him.

(12) The light in the sun that illuminates the whole world, that which is in the moon, that which is in the fire — know that light to be Mine.

(13) And permeating the earth, I maintain the beings by My energy, and nourish all the plants by becoming *Soma* (moon-god possessing the nectar of immortality also called *Soma*) and supplying the juice to them.

(14) Having become the digestive fire, I dwell in the bodies of the beings, and associating with the incoming and outgoing systems (of digestion) of the body, digest the four kinds of food (drunk, chewed, licked, and sucked).

(15) And I am seated in the hearts of all; from Me come memory, knowledge, as well as their loss; I am verily the one to be known through the study of the Vedas; indeed, I am the compiler of Vedanta (Upanishads), and I am the knower of the Vedas.

(16) There are two kinds of persons in this world — the perishable and the imperishable. All beings are perishable; but those situated in oneness of God consciousness are imperishable.

(17) But distinct is the Supreme Person spoken of as being the Highest Self, the Imperishable Lord, who permeates and maintains the three worlds (the higher heavenly worlds, the middle earthy worlds, and the lower hellish worlds).

(18) Since I am transcendental to the perishable (the spiritually unconscious beings), and even higher than the imperishable (the spiritually conscious beings situated in oneness with the Supreme), therefore I am well-known in the world and in the Vedas as Purushuttama (the Supreme Person).

(19) Whosoever, being undeluded, thus knows Me as Purushuttama, he, the all-knowing, worships Me with his whole being, O descendant of Bharata.

(20) Thus, this most secret science has been told by Me to you, O Anagha; understanding this, one becomes wise and has his duties fulfilled, O descendant of Bharata.

Although the limited capacities of our material senses make it difficult for us humans to experience God in all aspects of existence, including our own bodies, this does not imply that the Lord is not present in those elements. Lord Krishna firmly emphasizes in this chapter that He is everything and hence is present everywhere. He pervades our entire bodies in the form of indestructible individual souls. He is the ruler of the senses and the supreme beneficiary of all joys.

We should know Krishna as the Supreme Person and make use of the senses provided by Him to attain liberation from this material world and reach the self-illuminated world of Krishna. Relinquishing all mundane material cravings and attachments, being situated in perfect knowledge of the Supreme Lord, being ever devoted to Him, remaining mentally the same in all conditions, we should keep striving to attain this divine goal of human life.

Chapter 16 - Divine and Demonic Natures

The Bhagavad Gita is basically a how-to manual for living a perfect life. And to live a perfect life, we need to develop the qualities that make our lives perfect. But before developing those traits, we need to be *aware* of the traits that we should strive to develop, and the ones we should avoid.

Lord Krishna has made our task very simple by telling us exactly what divine qualities we need to have in order to live an ideal life in this material world, as well as the demonic characteristics we must escape at all costs.

So, what exactly are those divine and demonic attributes? Let's see.

Lord Krishna (to Arjuna):

(1) Fearlessness, purity of heart, knowledge, steadfastness in Yoga, charity, and control over the senses, performance of religious sacrifice, study of the holy scriptures, austerity, straightforwardness, ...

(2) ... non-injury (to the innocent), truthfulness, absence of anger, renunciation, peacefulness, aversion to slander, kindness to beings, absence of greed, gentleness, modesty, absence of restlessness, …

(3) … vigor, forgiveness, fortitude, purity, absence of hatred, absence of conceit — these attributes belong to one who is born to attain divine nature, O descendant of Bharata.

(4) Pride, arrogance, conceit, anger, and also harshness and ignorance — these attributes belong to one who is born to attain demonic nature, O Partha.

(5) The divine attributes are for liberation, the demonic attributes are considered to be for bondage. Do not grieve, O Pandava, for you are born with divine attributes.

(6) There are two kinds of created beings in this world — the divine and the demonic. The divine have been spoken of at great length; hear from Me, O Partha, of the demonic.

(7) People of demonic nature know not what is to be done and what is not to be done. Neither purity, nor good conduct, nor truthfulness exist in them.

(8) They say, "the universe is a lie, has no basis (of morality), has no God; it is brought about not by a systematic causal sequence, but by passionate desire (for union with the opposite sex); what else could be the cause?"

(9) Holding this view, the ruined souls of little intelligence engage in fierce and destructive activities harmful for the world.

(10) Taking refuge in insatiable lust, being absorbed in vanity, pride, and conceit, holding evil ideas due to delusion, they act in impure motivation.

(11) Fully engrossed in immeasurable cares (worldly and bodily cares and concerns) which have an end in death, regarding gratification of desires as the highest (goal of life), feeling sure that this is all, ...

(12) ... being bound by hundreds of shackles of hope (desire), giving themselves to lust and anger, they strive to amass wealth through dishonest means for sensual enjoyments.

(13) "This has been gained by me today; this object of desire I shall gain tomorrow; this is already there with me; and this wealth shall also be mine; ...

(14) ... that enemy has been killed by me already; I shall kill others too; I am the lord; I am the enjoyer; I am perfect, powerful, and happy; ...

(15) ... I am rich and well-born; who else is there like me? I will perform sacrifices (to please the gods and demand desire-fulfillment from them). I will do charity (for the same reason). I will rejoice." Thus they are deluded by ignorance.

(16) Bewildered by numerous thoughts (of desire fulfillment), entangled in the snare of delusion, and engrossed in the enjoyment of sense-gratification, they sink into a foul hell.

(17) Self-conceited, stubborn, intoxicated by pride in wealth, they perform sacrifice in name only, with ostentation, without following the scriptural injunctions.

(18) Given to ego, power, arrogance, lust, and anger, these malicious people hate Me in the bodies of their own and also of others.

(19) I hurl forever those cruel haters, the worst among men in the material world, the evil-doers, verily, into demonic wombs (in their coming lives).

(20) Entering demonic wombs (being born in demonic species) birth after birth, the fools (the ignorant ones), not attaining Me, O Kaunteya, reach even lower conditions (species).

(21) This gate of hell, destructive of the self (degrading the soul to the lowest species), is of three kinds — lust, anger, and greed. Therefore, one should abandon these three.

(22) O Kaunteya, a man who is free from these three gates to darkness strives for the good of the soul; thus, he attains the supreme goal (the eternal association of God).

(23) He who, ignoring the regulations of the scriptures, acts under the impulse of lust, neither attains perfection (of human existence), nor happiness, nor the supreme goal.

(24) Therefore, the scriptures are your guide in determining what should be done and what should not be done. You should act here knowing the regulations declared in the scriptures.

This chapter is very significant from a spiritual seeker's perspective in that it contains comprehensive lists of traits he can strive to develop and avoid in order to make himself fit for liberation. This chapter acts as a compass for every Yogi, and anyone who reads it on a regular basis will never be lost in his spiritual pursuits.

It is not difficult to notice that most, if not all, the divine and demonic characteristics stated by the Lord are already well-known to us as good and bad, respectively. Our God-given heart already understands which one is a desirable quality and which one is not. It's only that our deluded minds don't always allow us to prioritize the positive qualities above the negative ones. And the kind Lord is well aware of this. So, in order to make our lives easier, He enumerates all of those qualities for us, so that we are never perplexed, and our thoughts are never deceived.

Therefore, we should strive to cultivate the desirous qualities enumerated by Krishna, and try to avoid the undesirable ones — lust, anger, and greed, in particular, as these have been defined by the Lord as the "three gates to darkness." These are the three worst tendencies in our hearts that lead us away from God. So, we must avoid falling for them at all costs.

Krishna has made our task as simple as possible for us. We now have no justification for not being able to find freedom from this dreadful existence. If we fail despite knowing all of this, the blame can only be ours.

Chapter 17 - The Three Kinds of Faith

We saw in Chapter 14 how this material world is kept running by Lord's material nature. The three modes of material nature — sattva, rajas, and tamas — purity, passion, and darkness — can be seen in all aspects of life. All we have to do is be willing to look for them. That is the test of our knowledge and wisdom.

Every moment of our lives is a result of the decisions we've made in the past, though it doesn't always look to be so. Our current situation is just a result of the choices that we've made, either in our current lives or in our previous lives. The wise ones would have chosen purity; the ones who were too attached to the worldly life would have chosen passion, and the foolish and ignorant ones would have chosen darkness. But each of our choices, no matter how trivial they may seem to be, has the attributes of one or more of these three. And the one among these three that rules our minds at the moment we abandon our bodies determines our fates.

In this chapter, Lord Krishna delves deeper into the specifics, instructing Arjuna on how to distinguish among these three modes when it comes to faith, food, sacrifice, austerity, and charity. Let's learn from the Lord.

Arjuna (to Lord Krishna):

(1) Those who, setting aside the regulations of the scriptures, perform sacrifice with faith — what is their state, O Krishna? Is it s*attva* (the mode of purity), *rajas* (the mode of passion), or *tamas* (the mode of darkness)?

Lord Krishna (to Arjuna):

(2) Threefold is the faith of the embodied beings, according to their own nature — *sattvic* (of the mode of purity), *rajasic* (of the mode of passion), and also *tamasic* (of the mode of darkness). Thus, hear about this.

(3) O descendant of Bharata, the faith of each is in accordance with his nature. This man (human being) is made up of faith; what his faith is, that verily is he.

(4) Those in the mode of purity worship the demigods; those in the mode of passion worship nature-spirits and ogres; and the others, those in the mode of darkness, worship the spirits and a host of ghosts.

(5) Those persons who undergo severe austerities not prescribed in the scriptures, given to ostentation and ego, impelled by the forces of lust and attachment, ...

(6) ... senselessly torturing all the elements situated in the body, verily, also Me, situated within the body — know them to be of demonic resolve.

(7) Also, the food which is dear to each person is of three kinds; so also sacrifice, austerity, and charity. Hear about these distinctions.

(8) Foods that increase the duration of life, purity, strength, health, happiness, and affection, that are succulent, oleaginous, enduring, and agreeable, are dear to those in the mode of purity.

(9) Foods that are bitter, sour, salty, very hot, pungent, dry, and burning, are dear to those in the mode of passion, producing sorrow, grief, and disease.

(10) Foods that are not properly cooked, tasteless, putrid, and stale, and also remnants (of food eaten by others), and impure food, are dear to those in the mode of darkness.

(11) The sacrifice offered by those who are devoid of desire for rewards, performed in accordance with the scriptural regulations, with a mental conviction that it must be performed as it is surely a duty, is in the mode of purity.

(12) But that sacrifice which is performed seeking reward, as also for ostentation, O highest one in the dynasty of Bharata, know that sacrifice to be in the mode of passion.

(13) They (wise men) consider the sacrifice performed without scriptural regulations, without distribution of food (offered in sacrifice), without chanting of hymns (Vedic verses), without offerings (to the priests), and without faith (in God), to be in the mode of darkness.

(14) Worship of the demigods, the twice-born (Brahmins), the spiritual masters, and the wise (those having knowledge of spiritual truths), purity, straightforwardness, celibacy, and non-injury, are said to be the "austerity of the body."

(15) Speech that is not agitating, and is truthful, pleasant, and beneficial, and the practice of the study of the scriptures, are said to be the "austerity of speech."

(16) Tranquility of the mind, gentleness, silence, self-control, purity of nature — these are said to be the "austerity of the mind."

(17) This threefold austerity practiced with transcendental faith by men devoid of desire for rewards, they (wise men) call being in the mode of purity.

(18) The austerity which is practiced for gaining good reception, honor, and worship, and verily, with ostentation, is here said to be in the mode of passion — and it is unstable and fleeting.

(19) That austerity which is practiced out of foolish intent of torture of oneself or destruction of others is said to be in the mode of darkness.

(20) The gift which is given knowing that it ought to be given (as a righteous duty), without an expectation of return, at a proper place and time (to make sure of its proper use), and to a worthy person — that gift is considered to be in the mode of purity.

(21) But that gift which is given with the aim of getting something in return, or again desiring some reward, and is given reluctantly, is considered to be in the mode of passion.

(22) That gift which is given at an improper place and time (which may be detrimental to its proper use), and to unworthy persons, or without respect, with disdain, is considered to be in the mode of darkness.

Darkness is all about ego, which holds one's consciousness tied to an illusory way of perceiving life and the world around it, preventing one from seeing beyond. Passion is all about enjoying the moment, forgetting where the 'joy' is taking one.

Purity is all about knowledge and wisdom — making all decisions consciously, considering their qualities and consequences, and making choices in complete awareness of how Krishna will look upon them. That's the key question — the shortcut to recognize and choose sattva over rajas and tamas — "Whether Krishna would love me for this?" What's the issue with thinking this way?

Most of us are habituated to choose passion over purity. That's how most of us get trained by our well-meaning parents and teachers, and the so-called self-help gurus. And some of us get so used to being in that mode that we don't even notice when we slip into the mode of darkness.

No matter how we've been living up to this point, we must realize that it's still not too late. We still have time to make amends. Let's live the remainder of our lives in a state of purity. Peace is awaiting us, and so is Krishna.

The Lord continues:

(23) '*Om* (the Supreme) - *Tat* (the Absolute) - *Sat* (the True, the Good, the Auspicious)' — this is considered to be the threefold designation of the Brahman (God). By that were created formerly the Brahmins, the Vedas, and the sacrificial rites.

(24) Therefore, the performances of sacrifice, charity, and austerity always begin with the utterance of "Om" by the followers of the Brahman, as prescribed in the scriptural regulations.

(25) Uttering "tat" without desiring rewards are the acts of sacrifice, austerity, as also the various acts of charity performed by the seekers of liberation.

(26) This word "sat" is used is the sense of 'reality' (truth) and of 'goodness.' And also, O Partha, the word "sat" is used in the sense of an auspicious act.

(27) Steadfastness in sacrifice, austerity, and charity is also called *sat*, and also the actions meant for these are, verily, referred to as *sat*.

(28) Whatever is offered in sacrifice, given in charity, and practiced as austerity, without faith, is said to be *asat* (false — the opposite of *sat*, truth), O Partha; it is of no use here (in this life) or hereafter (after this life).

Sat, which literally means 'truth,' is what God is — the only truth in the universe. Lord Krishna is both the origin and the end of everything in the universe. He *is* the universe. Despite that, He is outside the universe. He is the supreme. He is the absolute one as well. He is the personification of purity, benevolence, and good fortune. He is the highest and the most immutable truth in all of existence.

And all of us are small fragments of that truth. We are not illusions or shadows, as believed by many philosophers. We are very real. But our reality is veiled by this packaging called the body. This body is the source of the illusion most of us live in. Let's realize this and immerse ourselves in that consciousness of reality.

Chapter 18 - Renunciation and Liberation

Lord Krishna has been exceedingly generous to us, the deluded humans born in the Kali-Yuga (the dark age), by disseminating the most profound knowledge in the universe in the form of His divine composition — the Bhagavad Gita.

The gracious Lord has disclosed all the secrets of a happy material life and a beautiful afterlife to us in the last seventeen chapters. And in this final chapter, He continues His instructions and discusses certain key principles before concluding His speech by summarizing all of His divine lessons so that we can make our way to Him in this realm of illusions with ease.

The first subject the Lord discusses in this final chapter is the often-misunderstood concept of renunciation.

Arjuna (to Lord Krishna):

(1) O mighty-armed, O Hrishikesha, O slayer of the demon Keshi, I wish to know distinctly the essence of *sannyasa* (the renounced order of life) and *tyaga* (renunciation).

Lord Krishna (to Arjuna):

(2) The learned ones know *sannyasa* to be the giving up of activities undertaken with desire. The wise call the giving up of the results of all activities as *tyaga*.

(3) Some philosophers say that all activities should be given up as evil; and others say that the activities of sacrifice, charity, and austerity should not be given up.

(4) O best among the descendants of Bharata, hear from Me the conclusion about renunciation. Renunciation, verily, O best among men, has been declared to be of three kinds.

(5) Acts of sacrifice, charity, and austerity should not be given up; they must surely be performed; for sacrifice, charity and austerity purify even the wise.

(6) But even these activities should be performed abandoning attachment and hankering for rewards. O Partha, this is My firm and best opinion.

(7) The renunciation of obligatory actions (by the ones who are yet to attain perfection in life) is not justifiable. The renunciation of them because of delusion is declared to be in the mode of darkness.

(8) He who, out of fear of bodily discomfort, renounces duty as it is painful, having performed renunciation in the mode of passion, surely does not obtain the reward of renunciation.

(9) Whatever obligatory action is performed merely because it ought to be done, O Arjuna, renouncing attachment and hankering for the reward, that renunciation is considered to be in the mode of purity.

(10) The man of renunciation, absorbed in the mode of purity, being intelligent, having doubts cut asunder, neither hates improper action, nor becomes attached to proper action.

(11) It is indeed not possible for the embodied beings to renounce actions entirely; but he who renounces the rewards of actions is called a man of renunciation.

(12) The threefold results of actions — evil, good, and mixed — accrue after death to those who are not renounced; but never to the *sannyasins* (the ones who follow a renounced order of life).

(13) O Mahabaho, learn from Me these five causes for the accomplishment of all actions, which have been spoken of in the Sankhya (Upanishad or Vedanta) — the end of all actions.

(14) The seat (the body), as also the doer, and the various kinds of instruments (sense organs, mind, intelligence), and the various kinds of efforts (the separate functions of the organs), and also the presiding deity (of the respective sense organs), here is the fifth (cause for the accomplishment of all actions).

(15) Whatever action a man performs by his body, speech, and mind — be it fair (right), or the opposite (unfair or wrong) — these five are its causes.

(16) This being the case, anyone who, due to his immature understanding, sees himself alone as the performer, he, of perverted intelligence, does not see things as they are.

(17) He who is not of egoistic nature, he whose intelligence is not tainted (and thus does not see himself as the performer of actions), he, though killing in this world, does not kill, nor becomes entangled (by such actions).

(18) Knowledge, the object of knowledge (God), and the knower form the threefold impetus to action; the instruments of action (senses), the action, and the performer of action are the three constituents of action.

The genuine meaning of renunciation has been perverted by lazy people who claim that the Lord wants all of us to give up work and just worship Him all of the time. However, the Lord has stated multiple times in the Bhagavad Gita that renunciation is not the same as inaction. Renunciation is the act of separating oneself from the desire for the benefits of one's deeds. In reality, it is impossible to stop taking action completely. We like it or not, we are bound to engage in some sort of activity. In fact, our bodies continue to act even while we are unaware of it.

In any case, one should never renounce the activities of making sacrifices, giving charity, and being austere. According to Krishna, these are the three activities that must never be abandoned.

All action is a united effort of the five elements of action, as stated by the Lord in verse 14. Therefore, one must take care never to egoistically consider oneself as the performer of activities. A man of knowledge sees things as they are. We are not the controllers, but are the controlled. We must be aware of this.

Of course, this should not be used as an excuse to engage in a variety of unethical behaviors while claiming that one is not the perpetrator and hence should not be held accountable. While nature is the real doer in this world, we nevertheless have control over which aspects of nature we adopt. As a result, we are totally responsible for our karma.

(19) Knowledge, and action, and the performer of action are declared to be of three kinds in the science of the modes of material nature, according to the distinctions of the modes (purity, passion, and darkness); hear about them also as they are.

(20) That by which one sees the one imperishable nature in all beings, undivided (Supreme Soul) in the divided (individual souls) — know that knowledge to be in the mode of purity.

(21) But that knowledge which perceives in all beings various entities of different kinds, distinct from one another — know that knowledge to be in the mode of passion.

(22) But that knowledge which is confined to one form (the body along with the senses), as if it were the whole, without reason, without foundation in truth, and trivial, is declared to be in the mode of darkness.

(23) That action which is regulated (done as an obligatory duty), free from attachment, which is done without attraction or repulsion, by one who does not hanker for the reward, is said to be in the mode of purity.

(24) But that action which is performed by one who longs for the fulfillment of his desires, or with ego (resulting from identifying oneself with the body), and with too much strain, is said to be in the mode of passion.

(25) That action which is undertaken out of delusion, without consideration of the possible loss, harm, consequences, and one's own ability, is said to be in the mode of darkness.

(26) The performer of action who is free from attachment, non-egoistic, endowed with firmness and enthusiasm (toward fulfillment of his duties in the manner approved in the scriptures), and unperturbed by success and failure, is said to be in the mode of purity.

(27) The performer of action who is attached, hankering for the reward of action, greedy, of injurious mentality, impure, and subject to joy and sorrow, is declared to be in the mode of passion.

(28) The performer of action who is unsteady, materialistic, stubborn, unscrupulous, malicious, lazy, morose, and procrastinating, is said to be in the mode of darkness.

(29) Hear the threefold classification of intelligence and also of fortitude, according to the *gunas* (the three modes of material nature), as I describe them elaborately and severally, O Dhananjaya.

(30) That which knows the paths of action and withdrawal, what ought to be done and what ought not to be done, fear and fearlessness, and bondage and liberation — that intelligence, O Partha, is in the mode of purity.

(31) That by which one wrongly understands righteousness and unrighteousness, and also what ought to be done and what ought not to be done — that intelligence, O Partha, is in the mode of passion.

(32) That which, enveloped in darkness, perceives unrighteousness and righteousness, and all other things, in a perverted way — that intelligence, O Partha, is in the mode of darkness.

(33) The fortitude, constantly held through Yoga (of meditation), by which one restrains the functions of the mind, life-breath, and senses — that fortitude, O Partha, is in the mode of purity.

(34) But the fortitude by which, O Arjuna, one holds on to duty, lust, and wealth, longing for rewards due to attachment — that fortitude, O Partha, is in the mode of passion.

(35) The fortitude by which an unintelligent person does not abandon day-dreaming (illusion), fear, grief, despondency, and also conceit — that fortitude, O Partha, is in the mode of darkness.

(36) But now hear from Me of the three kinds of happiness, O best among the descendants of Bharata, where one rejoices by practice, and attains the end of sorrow.

(37) That which is like poison in the beginning, but comparable to nectar in the end, that, born of the purity of one's own intelligence, is said to be happiness in the mode of purity.

(38) That which is like nectar in the beginning, but comparable to poison in the end, that, born of the contact of the senses-organs with the sense-objects, is considered to be happiness in the mode of passion.

(39) That which, both in the beginning as also in the end, deludes oneself, that, born of sleep, laziness, and heedlessness, is said to be happiness in the mode of darkness.

(40) There is no being on earth, or again among the demigods in heaven, who is free from the three modes of material nature.

The world we live in is one of deception. Some say we're the ones in charge. Some believe God is in charge. However, neither is totally correct. The quality of our thoughts is the only thing we have control over. God's control is also limited because this material world is created, destroyed, and maintained by a fragment of His opulence. In other words, the Lord entrusts the upkeep of this planet to that fragment, and it acts on behalf of the Lord. And the name of that fragment is Prakriti — material nature.

Lord Krishna, in the previous chapters, has already revealed how His material nature maintains the functions of the entire world by being present in all elements of it. This is crucial information for us to comprehend as material beings. And that is why, in this final chapter too, Krishna instructs us how we can separate knowledge, action, performer of action, intelligence, fortitude, and happiness into the three modes of material nature — the modes of purity, passion, and darkness.

It is critical that we understand these distinctions because only then will we be able to progress through these modes and, eventually, transcend them to reach Krishna.

Next, the Lord educates us about our prescribed duties as follows.

(41) O Parantapa, the duties of the Brahmins (the religious scholars), the Kshatriyas (the royal warriors and protectors), the Vaishyas (the merchants), and the Shudras (the laborers) are allocated according to the qualities born of their own material nature.

(42) The duties of Brahmins, born of their own nature, are serenity, self-control, austerity, purity, forgiveness, as also straightforwardness, knowledge, realization, and faith.

(43) The duties of Kshatriyas, born of their own nature, are valor, splendor, firmness, skillfulness, and also not fleeing from battle, generosity, and lordliness.

(44) The duties of Vaishyas, born of their own nature, are agriculture, cattle-rearing, and trade. And, the duty of Shudras, born of their own nature, is in the form of service.

(45) Devoted to his own duty (born of his own nature), each man attains perfection. How devoted to his own duty he attains perfection — hear that.

(46) From whom all beings arise, by whom all this is pervaded, worshipping Him with his own duty (by being devoted to his own duty), a man attains perfection.

(47) Superior is one's own duty, though it may be devoid of merits, than the duty of another well-performed. One who performs the duty prescribed by one's own nature does not incur sin.

(48) O Kaunteya, one should not abandon the duty with which one is born, even though it may be faulty; for, verily, all undertakings are surrounded with faults, as fire with smoke.

(49) One whose intelligence is unattached everywhere, whose mind is under his control, who is devoid of desires, attains through *sannyasa* (the renounced order of life) the supreme perfection of freedom from action.

This is the final set of instructions given in the Bhagavad Gita by Lord Krishna. The qualities existing in one's character are what dictate his prescribed duties, and not the womb from which he emerges in the world. Prahlada was the son of a demon, but his character had the qualities of a devotee. To this day, the sages regard Prahlada as a devotee of the highest order. The fourfold social classification prevalent in ancient times no longer exists in the Kali-Yuga. But we can take cues from the attributes gifted to us by nature and choose our paths in the material life accordingly. This is indeed a mandatory prerequisite for both material as well as spiritual success.

One should strive to remain fixed in one's own duty, and not get lured by others' duties, seeing them getting success. No work is meant to be undertaken by all. It is something important for us to bear in mind when deciding on our career paths, as that has a direct impact on our spiritual advancement as well.

In the following verses, the Lord summarizes all His important teachings with the aim of making sure we do not miss out on any of His crucial messages. The following verses contain all the dos and don'ts for a Yogi striving to attain perfection, leading to his deliverance from this world and admission into Krishna's supreme abode, where he would live serving the Lord of all lords blissfully and perpetually.

(50) How one, achieving perfection, also attains the Brahman (the Supreme God), O Kaunteya, understand for certain from Me, in brief, that supreme state of knowledge.

(51) Absorbed in a fully purified intellect, and regulating oneself by firmness, renouncing sense-objects such as sound, and abandoning attachment and repulsion (to such sense-objects), ...

(52) ... dwelling in solitude, eating lightly, having speech, body, and mind under control, being ever absorbed in Dhyana Yoga (Yoga of meditation), having taken refuge in dispassion, ...

(53) ... having abandoned ego, power, pride, lust, anger, and accumulation of material possessions, being freed from the notion of ownership, and hence peaceful, one becomes fit to become one with the Brahman.

(54) Being one with the Brahman, blissful in the self (the knowledge of being a soul), he neither grieves nor desires. Being the same to all beings, he gains supreme devotion toward Me.

(55) By devotion, he knows Me in essence — what and who I am. Then, knowing Me in essence, he enters into Me immediately.

(56) Although ever engaged in all kinds of activities, taking shelter in Me, he, by My grace, attains the eternal, imperishable state (of liberation).

(57) Mentally renouncing all actions in Me, considering Me as the supreme, taking refuge in Yoga of discrimination (knowledge), keep your consciousness ever fixed on Me.

(58) Having your consciousness fixed on Me, you will cross over all obstacles by My grace; but if, out of ego, you do not listen to My teachings, you will be destroyed (by falling into the vicious cycle of birth and death).

(59) If, taking refuge in ego (leading to the false belief that one is the doer), you think, "I will not fight," vain is this resolve of yours; for your material nature will impel you.

(60) Bound by your own duties born of your own nature, O Kaunteya, that which you do not want to do, out of illusion, even that you shall helplessly do.

(61) The Lord dwells in the heart-region of all beings, O Arjuna, causing all beings, by the spell of His illusions (material nature), to revolve, as if mounted on a machine.

(62) O descendant of Bharata, take refuge in Him alone with your whole being. By His grace, you will attain the supreme peace (of liberation), and the eternal abode.

(63) This knowledge, more secret than any other secret, has been imparted to you by Me. Reflecting on this fully, act as per your desire.

(64) Listen again to My supreme word, the most confidential of all. Because you are very dear to Me, therefore, I will tell you what is beneficial for you.

(65) Fix your mind upon Me; become My devotee; sacrifice unto Me; bow down to Me; thus, you will surely come to Me. Truth do I promise to you, for you are dear to Me.

(66) Abandoning all forms of engagements (unnecessary material and religious activities), take refuge in Me alone. I will liberate you from all sins. Do not grieve.

This is what all the wisdom bestowed upon us by Lord Krishna culminates into. The summation of right knowledge (of the soul and the Supreme Soul), right action (without desire for rewards), right meditation (on the Lord alone), and right devotion (exclusively to the Lord) is a sure-shot recipe for perfection in this world and liberation in the next. But each of these forms of Yoga must be understood to perfection by the Yogi. Also, it must be understood that these are not separate mutually exclusive paths leading to Krishna. These should be viewed as the different components of Yogic perfection. The absence of any of these invariably results in failure.

Now, let us see what the Lord says regarding the divine significance of the wisdom provided by Him in the Bhagavad Gita, who deserves to gain this and who should ever remain oblivious to it, who has the authority to impart it to others, and what the study of it can lead to.

(67) This (the knowledge that Krishna has provided herein) should not ever be taught by you to one who is not austere, and to one who is not a devotee, not also to one who does not render service, nor as well to one who cavils at Me.

(68) He who, with utmost devotion to Me, will teach this supreme secret of Mine to My devotees will certainly come to Me without doubt.

(69) And no one else is there among men who does dearer service to Me than him, nor will there ever be another dearer to Me than him in this world.

(70) And he who will study this sacred conversation of ours, I shall have been worshipped by him by the sacrifice of gaining knowledge; such is My opinion.

(71) A man who hears this, full of faith and free from disdain, he too, being liberated, attains to the auspicious planets of the doers of righteous deeds.

The Lord confirms that this holy wisdom should never be divulged to a non-believer or non-devotee. Only an open-minded individual with a curious attitude who is willing to listen attentively to the divine instructions and does not use flimsy doubts as an excuse to ignore its lessons is qualified to plunge into this pure and divine wisdom.

Studying the Bhagavad Gita is equal to worshipping the Lord. And whoever reads it regularly and follows all of its instructions would surely reach Krishna. Even better, if a devotee of the Lord achieves perfection through the study and application of this knowledge, and also shares this wisdom with others who deserve to be blessed with it, he rises even higher in Krishna's eyes.

After emphasizing the significance of His song, the blessed Lord poses the following question to Arjuna:

(72) Has this (all that Krishna has taught) been heard by you, O Partha, with a single-pointed mind? Has your delusion, caused by ignorance, been destroyed, O Dhananjaya?

And Arjuna replies:

Arjuna (to Lord Krishna):

(73) O Achyuta, my delusion is destroyed, and my memory (about one's true identity) has been regained by me through Your grace. I am firmly situated; my doubts are gone. I will now act according to Your word.

This is enlightenment. Anyone who studies Krishna's discourse with a pure heart will undoubtedly become enlightened, as Arjuna did. Anyone who acts in accordance with His word will undoubtedly be able to reach Him. This is an irrefutable fact.

Sanjaya (to Dhritarashtra):

(74) Thus, I have heard this wonderful dialogue between Vasudeva (Krishna) and the great-souled Partha (Arjuna), which causes the hair on the body to stand on end with joy.

(75) Through the grace of Vyasa (who provided Sanjaya with the divine power to witness and hear this sacred conversation), I have heard this supreme secret Yoga directly from Krishna, the Lord of Yoga, Himself revealing it.

(76) O King, recalling and recalling again this wonderful and sacred dialogue between Keshava (Krishna) and Arjuna, I rejoice again and again.

(77) And recalling and recalling again that extremely wonderful form of Hari (Krishna's universal form), great is my amazement, O King; and I rejoice again and again.

(78) Where there is Krishna, the Lord of Yoga, and where there is Partha, the great wielder of bow, there are prosperity, victory, power, and firm policy; such is my opinion.

Sanjaya is someone who any sincere Yogi would be envious of (of course, in a good way). He was only a charioteer of Dhritarashtra. But he must have had some really great karma on his side that he got the opportunity to witness the most divine conversation as and when it was happening. It is difficult to imagine the joy he would have experienced hearing this enlightening dialogue between the best of students and the greatest of masters.

But that does not mean we should consider ourselves unfortunate. We still have the holy guide with us that can help us live a blissful and successful life. We have the word of God with us, which is nothing but Krishna Himself in the form of a song.

Read it. Read it again. Read till you understand it to the core. Read till its teachings become second nature to you. Be Arjuna. Be Sanjaya. Be enlightened. Be liberated.

Conclusion

What can a servitor of the Lord say to conclude His holy word that is grand enough to match its sheer magnificence? Nothing.

So, I will just share a few suggestions of my own. I urge you to consider these as requests.

Look. It's really easy to find flaws even in God's word. We, as humans, are masters at instilling doubt. I'm not implying that it's a bad thing. Being cautious is always advisable. However, doing so with prejudice in order to prove something incorrect simply because it appears to be too difficult to comprehend and follow is dumb.

Again, most of us approach the Bhagavad Gita from a philosophical standpoint. Of course, it's a philosophy and should be considered as one. But it's important to remember that it's not *just* a philosophy. Studying it for knowledge and then uttering its verses to boast of one's 'knowledge' does not help. We must realize that it is a philosophy *to live by*, to practice, and not just to study and preach.

That is why, in the Bhagavad Gita, Lord Krishna outlines the process in such detail. Gather knowledge. But don't stop there. Realizing the authority and essence of Krishna, meditate on Him. Dedicate all of your work to Him. And then reach the pinnacle of perfection by surrendering to Him.

While doing so, the biggest obstacle for you would be your own ego. The word 'surrender' itself bothers us, because it hurts our ego. "I have a personality of my own. Why should I surrender to somebody else?" It's a pity that we have no qualms about surrendering to our bosses, customers, or anyone else who we have something to gain from or who is in a more powerful position than us. But we have issues surrendering to God. The reason? We don't 'see' God (at least we believe so); so, we don't have enough faith in His existence and opulence.

Remember what Krishna says: "O Kaunteya, I am the taste of water; I am the light of the moon and the sun; I am the syllable "Om" in all the Vedas; the sound in space; and virility in men." [BG 7.8] Can't we see water, the sun, and the moon?

The Lord asserts multiple times throughout the Bhagavad Gita that He is everywhere and in everything. If we don't perceive Him, it does not mean He's not there. It is our own ignorance that prevents us from seeing Him.

Rise above your ego. Rise above your limiting thought patterns. Rise above the illusion. Do not remain lost.

Keep things simple. Start by realizing who you are. Body? Mind? Spirit? Then understand that other beings are the same as you.

Then realize God. Who is He, exactly? How does He look? Where does He live? What are His abilities? What are His characteristics?

Then seek the knowledge about your purpose. Why are you here? To gather things? For having fun? Or do you have a higher goal in life to achieve? How can you achieve your goal?

Krishna sung the Bhagavad Gita to Arjuna. Sanjaya retold the exact same words as spoken by the Lord to Dhritarashtra. Arjuna attained enlightenment. Dhritarashtra, on the other hand, did not learn anything. The choice is yours. Who would you prefer to be? Do you choose to be closed-minded and materially attached like Dhritarashtra? Or do you choose to be an enlightened devotee like Arjuna? There is no third choice.

If you choose to be Arjuna your task is rather straightforward. Simply put yourself in Arjuna's shoes, and talk to God through the Bhagavad Gita. Read a few verses of the Bhagavad Gita whenever you want to talk to God. They are ignorant who ask, "Why doesn't God speak to us?" He speaks to each of us in every moment. We just don't listen.

Krishna keeps asking us, "Has this (all that Krishna has taught) been heard by you, O Partha, with a single-pointed mind? Has your delusion, caused by ignorance, been destroyed, O Dhananjaya?" [BG 18.72]

Keep reading this song of God until you can recite the following words of Arjuna to Him: "O Achyuta, my delusion is destroyed, and my memory (about one's true identity) has been regained by me through Your grace. I am firmly situated; my doubts are gone. I will now act according to Your word." [BG 18.73]

May Krishna bless all!

About the Author

Hari Chetan is a spiritual and consciousness coach and has an immense amount of experience in the fields of religion, spirituality, theology, and ancient and modern philosophy. He is an expert in all major religions and spiritual philosophies including Christianity, Hinduism, Islam, Buddhism, Sikhism, Jainism, Judaism, Stoicism, Zen, Taoism, and Baha'i. However, Vedic philosophy is his primary area of interest.

Having discovered the oldest and most confidential spiritual wisdom contained in the Vedic scriptures, Hari is on a mission to spread this knowledge to all corners of the globe. His goal is to awaken the entire world to the true identity of the self and God, and make everyone aware of the purpose of their existence, as this is the only lasting solution to all our problems. He currently lives in Kolkata, India with his family.

Connect with Hari Chetan:

harichetan.com
hari@harichetan.com
facebook.com/HariChetanOfficial

A Gift for You

In the daily commotion that characterizes our lives nowadays, it is quite easy to lose track of oneself. And so it is important for us to maintain our mental equilibrium by connecting with our spiritual selves on a regular basis.

Download Hari Chetan's **free Bhagavad Gita Workbook** designed especially for the readers of his books.

This workbook will help you test your knowledge of the core concepts given in the Bhagavad Gita, and to keep you on track in your spiritual journey.

Try it. It's free to download and is very useful!

Visit **www.harichetan.com** to download.

The Bhagavad Gita Series

Book 1: Bhagavad Gita - The Perfect Philosophy: 15 Reasons That Make the Song of God the Most Scientific Ideology

Book 2: Bhagavad Gita (in English): The Authentic English Translation for Accurate and Unbiased Understanding

Book 3: 30 Days to Understanding the Bhagavad Gita: A Complete, Simple, and Step-by-Step Guide to the Million-Year-Old Confidential Knowledge

Book 4: The Bhagavad Gita Summarized and Simplified: A Comprehensive and Easy-to-Read Summary of the Divine Song of God

Book 5: Mind Management through the Bhagavad Gita: Master your Mindset in 21 Days and Discover Unlimited Happiness and Success

All Books: Bhagavad Gita (In English) – The Complete Collection: 5-Books-in-1

Read Next ...

If you enjoyed reading this English translation of the Bhagavad Gita, I recommend reading *30 Days to Understanding the Bhagavad Gita*, the next book in the Bhagavad Gita series.

If you've read the Bhagavad Gita in its entirety, you'll know that it spans eighteen chapters and covers a variety of topics, each of which is spread over multiple chapters. It is not structured in such a way that each chapter focuses on a single topic, but rather includes a lot of (well-intended) repetition. This often makes it pretty difficult for the seeker to keep track of the various topics and to design a comprehensive learning approach.

Reading the Bhagavad Gita verse-by-verse is obviously necessary as a first step in understanding its philosophy. However, for a genuine seeker who wants to truly comprehend this philosophy and use it in his life, having a guide that contains all of this material separated by topics for easy learning, retention, and reference is essential. That is where *30 Days to Understanding the Bhagavad Gita* comes in handy.

This book is designed as a comprehensive 30-day program that will help you grasp one topic each day. It breaks down the timeless wisdom contained in the Bhagavad Gita into easily digestible bites. It takes the reader on a spiritual journey through a step-by-step approach in which each topic builds on the previous one and all the elements come together to form an enlightening image in the end.

Visit **www.harichetan.com/books** to learn more about the book.